Kitchen Primer
Dinner's Ready

Instructor's Guide

By
Laurie Zerga

For Chef-K®

Kitchen Primer Dinner's Ready Instructor's Guide

2018

Laurie Zerga, founder
Chef-K
www.chef-k.com
info@chef-k.com

Some portions of this course material have been obtained from public sources or by permission. The following is a list of sources from which this material has been drawn:

- Federal Drug Administration
- National Science Teachers Association (NSTA)
- United States Department of Agriculture (USDA)
- United States Department of Health and Human Services (HHS)

Table of Contents

Introduction

Camp Overview

This program focuses on simple, familiar menus. You will learn to prepare traditional entrees that are tasty and nutritious. As always there is a focus on seasonal ingredients.

By the end of the week, you will have covered basic food preparation, reading recipes, cooking, and cleanup.

Day/date	Mon	Tues	Wed	Thurs	Fri
Hour 0	Instructor setup	Instructor setup	Instructor setup	Instructor setup	Instructor setup
Hour 1	Intro and Knife Skills	Food Safety Sauté & Browning Technique	Sum of the Parts	Food Allergies What's in the Oven?	Celebration and certificates
	Let's Make Salad Entrée	It's not just a Hamburger	Everyone likes Pasta	Basic Roasted Meal	Mexican Fiesta Menu
Hour 2	Menu Prep	Menu Prep	Menu Prep	Menu Prep	Prep
	Lunch	Lunch	Lunch	Lunch	Lunch
Hour 3	Cleanup	Cleanup	Cleanup	Cleanup	Cleanup
	Day ends	Day ends	Day ends	Day ends	Day ends
	Instructor cleanup	Instructor cleanup	Instructor cleanup	Instructor cleanup	Instructor cleanup
	Menu	Menu	Menu	Menu	Menu
	Seasonal Vegetable Salad with Chicken	Salisbury steak with French Onion Sauce	Pasta with Red & Green Sauce	Oven Roasted Chicken	Turkey Tacos
	Fresh Fruit	Rice	Simple Salad	Roasted Potatoes & Vegetables	Guacamole & Salsa
		Sautéed Zucchini	Green Beans	Fresh Fruit	Calabacitas (vegetables)
		Fresh Fruit	Fresh Fruit		Fresh Fruit

The class can accommodate up to 16 students. It provides you with tasting, tactile and hands on experience. Each day includes lesson handouts and recipes for your future reference.

Generally, Chef-K® classes ensure that participants understand the importance of seasonal ingredients, particularly produce such as fruit and vegetables. Appendixes A and B have a general list of fruit and vegetables available by season.

The instructor or an assistant will have to shop for ingredients for the recipes prior to each class. Produce should be as fresh as possible, so the shopping should not be done too many days in advance. Each class will include a shopping list for food as well as a list of the tools and utensils needed to set up the class.

Note: It is recommended that parents be invited for Friday's celebration. Determine if this is a possibility with the camp facility staff. If it is; coordinate to invite parents for Friday.

Class materials

Instructors have been provided with the overall instructor's guide as well as the participant handouts. We have provided a "Check what You've Learned" in Appendix C for use on the last day. We've also included a survey for both the instructor and participants. Chef-K will request that a formal survey be returned from both the instructor and the class assistant for each course once it's complete. We would like to see any surveys returned by course participants as well. Participant evaluations can be found in Appendix J.

Instructor surveys, certificate of completion and other activities are provided to instructors electronically.

Class size

Depending upon the experience of the instructor in working with food and children, the number of participants that can be accommodated will vary. It is possible to have one instructor for up to twelve middle school participants or teens. As a general guideline, plan on one instructor to handle a maximum of eight children, ages seven to twelve, and up to twelve participants, ages twelve to seventeen. Plan on an assistant for each additional four children, ages seven to twelve, and for each additional six children, ages twelve to seventeen. Assistants should be familiar with reading a recipe and have a general comfort level in the kitchen. An assistant is very important when considering participant safety during class. The assistant also should be able to answer simple questions and help the instructor keep the class running smoothly. In addition, assistants shorten preparation and cleanup time. Sometimes older club members or members of the community will volunteer to help. Throughout the document, recommendations are made for what tasks might be assigned to an assistant.

Number of instructors	Instructor's experience	Age of participants	Recommended number of participants per instructor	Number of assistants needed for additional participants
1	Experienced children's cooking instructor	7-11	8	1 for 9-12 participants 2 for over 12 participants*
1	Experienced children's cooking instructor	12-17	12	1 assistant if over 12 teens

*Usually 1 instructor and an assistant are sufficient for up to 15 participants; however, an especially young group may require a second assistant for lessons such as knife skills. Ask if someone is available to help.

Participant groups

Chef-K staff members have found that it works well to divide participants into groups when they are working on the exercises during lessons and when they are following and completing recipes. Dividing the participants into groups is particularly useful when they are required to follow the recipes in this course because they are held accountable for understanding how to follow the recipe. As a side benefit, following recipes is excellent reading practice. Groups of about four seem to be the best size to prepare these recipes.

It is important to have enough tools available so that each group has its own set. An overall list of tools needed for all classes is included in Appendix E and in the instructor's guide for each class.

Tips for the instructor

- Develop a relationship with produce managers at local markets. Often, they will discount produce for use in classes.
- Some ingredients may be available through local food banks. Ensure that the food is fresh and that the use-by or expiration date has not passed.
- Select fruit and vegetables for the recipes that are the most fresh and free of bruises or spots.
- Select fruit and vegetables in surprising colors. Select blood oranges in the winter that have deep burgundy flesh inside instead of the typical orange color. Rainbow carrots or Easter radishes are often available in the spring. Bring in different-colored apples.
- It's easiest to find unusual fruit and vegetables at farmers' markets, natural food stores, or specialty grocers.
- Let the children help wash the produce during class when there is time.

Preparation and Logistics

Before each class

Use a signup sheet (provided electronically to instructors) to keep track of participants. In order to calculate the copies that you need, plan to divide class into groups of 4.

1. Print one copy of the handouts for each participant and put the handouts at each participant's work area.
2. For each group of participants, print an additional copy of the recipes and put in plastic sleeves for each group. The plastic sleeves will protect the recipes for the participants to take home.

Either you or your assistant must prepare the room before each class.

Setting Up tables in the general preparation room

The number of tables that you will need depends on the space available and on the number of participants. If your facility has a kitchen or snack area, you can use those countertops. Tables are a better height for younger children, and countertops are a better height for teenagers.

If you are using an all-purpose room, use one table for staging and to set up supplies, tools, and ingredients.

For the participant work area, allow about 24 inches per participant. A typical 8-foot table can accommodate eight participants and an instructor at the end of the table, who can then demonstrate techniques to the participants. Put four participants on each side of the table. If you have 16 participants, you will need two tables.

Note: If you have 16 participants, aged 7 to 12, you must have two assistants. One assistant can sit at the end of the second table to demonstrate techniques.

Preparing the workspace for participants

Using an antibacterial cleaner, wipe off the stove, sink, countertops, tables, and all work surfaces.

Cover the work surfaces with a plastic tablecloth, if needed. For example, you may need to use this if there is an old folding table that is used for art projects, etc.

Put a cutting mat at each participant's work area.

Either set out a dishpan or choose an area near a sink where participants can put dirty dishes.

Preparing produce

Pre-wash the produce for participants. However, when there is time let participants help wash produce. Ask them about washing in hot or cold water. Would they give a flower hot or cold water? A vegetable or fruit is kind of like that, so wash it in cold water.

Be aware of your kitchen oven space. If the oven space is limited, you may need to switch the green bean recipe on Wednesday to Thursday's menu. And then do the roasted vegetables on Wednesday instead of green beans.

A note about using fruit for dessert: If there is time you can consider doing fun things with extra fruit or vegetables. The kids really enjoy "making up recipes". Here are some samples that can be integrated into the class if there is extra time; particularly if the participants are middle school or high school age. And of course, some kitchens, may not have the tools or appliances; however if you have a fully stocked kitchen tool set these are nice extras.

1) If you have plenty of bananas you can cut them into 1-inch chunks and freeze them. Then puree them in a food processor or blender. Serve like ice cream with berries on top.
2) Apples can be peeled, sliced and baked with just 2 Tbsp of brown sugar and some extra nuts and 2 Tbsp of butter or olive oil, or a bit extra whole wheat flour.
3) Extra onion sauce, tomatoes, and rice can be re-heated together for Friday. Add some cumin and chili powder for a Spanish-rice side dish.

Assembling ingredients for each group

For each group, put all recipe ingredients on a tray or in a pan—such as a metal-rimmed cookie sheet or large baking pan—on the staging table. Each group will take a tray or pan to their assigned work area. This teaches the importance of assembling all ingredients before starting to prepare food.

Assembling tools and appliances for each group

For each group, put a set of the kitchen tools needed for each recipe on the staging table.

Daily menus require a stove; ensure cook top and oven are functioning prior to start of the camp. Always check the oven prior to pre-heating it for preparing any recipe; since people sometimes use it for storage rather than cooking.

During class

Important: Always be aware of potential dangers to participants (such as knives and heat). Do not leave participants unsupervised.

Schedule for a 3-hour class

The following table contains an example of an ideal 3-hour class schedule. The actual time will vary, based on the group dynamics and the number of participants, participants' age, skill level, and so on. Generally, the first two or three classes tend to run late. As the week progresses, participants become more confident and are able to complete recipes more quickly.

30 to 45 minutes for the lesson	Discuss the handouts with the participants and have them fill out the assessments (Check What You Know and Check What You've Learned) in the handouts.
1 hour for recipe preparation	Oversee and mentor participants while they prep the ingredients.
30 minutes for recipe assembly, cooking, meal setup, and serving	Set the table for buffet or plate serving. Choose a serving approach that is appropriate for the menu. Use your discretion.
20 minutes to eat	Have participants sit down together and taste what they have made. Sit with them, ask what they like, ask what they have not tasted before, and thank them for trying something new.
20 minutes for cleanup	Have participants clear their dishes. Have participants clean their work area and wash the dishes until the class ends.

General information and rules

The primary goal of this course is to instruct participants in basic kitchen skills, including reading recipes, handling food and kitchen tools safely, and learning cooking techniques. The instructor and assistant will oversee the participants practicing their skills and will, only rarely, do a task for them. It's important to review general kitchen etiquette and discuss appropriate behavior expected during class. Here are some general examples and rules that should always be observed:

1. Children should remove outdoor jackets and roll up long sleeves.
2. Children should place long hair in a pony tail. This is to ensure that hair does not get into the food. Consider having a pack of hair bands to give to any participants who need them.
3. Children should not chew gum, drink or eat near the food preparation area.
4. All cell phones should be silent.
5. Children should wash their hands. Tell them that it is always important to wash their hands before handling food. Ask them if they know why they wash their hands. Ideally this topic has been discussed in the past so they will be familiar with proper hand washing. If not, here are the proper steps:

- Roll long sleeves up to the elbow.
- Wet hands with warm water.
- Remove hands from water and add a small amount of soap.
- Rub soap all over hands, including front and back, between fingers, and up to wrists for twenty to thirty seconds. Singing "Happy Birthday" or "Row, Row, Row your Boat" two times takes about the right amount of time.
- Rinse with warm water and dry with a paper towel or air dry.

6. If a participant is too young to use a knife, the assistant will help him or her do other tasks required to complete the recipe. These may include reading the recipe, identifying ingredients, peeling, tearing, blending, whisking, or other tasks that do not require a knife.
7. It's easiest to split a large group into small groups. Groups of three to four work very well.
8. Make sure each child has a cutting mat. This will define space for each child and provide an extra layer of clean surface.
9. Pass out the trays with ingredients for each recipe when it's time to begin making the recipe.
10. Let the participants read the recipe and mix the ingredients.
11. Most classes contain a game plan to follow for preparing the recipe. Often a specific order is recommended in order to limit the risk of cross contamination.
12. Try to let each participant take a turn at working with the ingredients. If you are working with particularly young children, here are some things they can do without having to use any sharp tools:
    - pulling the seeds out of a bell pepper
    - pulling the strings off a piece of celery
    - snapping the stem off a radish
    - pulling the string from a pea pod
    - breaking apart broccoli florets
13. Think of ways to engage the participants. Have them try smelling, tasting, and touching unfamiliar ingredients.
14. Try to always have the participants arrange the food on a platter or in a bowl. Give suggestions on ways to make it look appealing like one might see in a cooking show. Add a little garnish.
15. When serving the food, often the instructor or the assistant will have to oversee distribution of the food. Many participants left in a buffet style line without guidance will take as much food as they can without regard for the others in the class. There will not be enough for everyone if the food is not monitored during serving. Once they have taken enough classes to understand portion control, this becomes less of an issue.

16. The assistant will gather any ingredients or tools needed by the instructor during class.
17. The instructor or an assistant will be with participants at all times.
18. While the instructor is overseeing the final cooking, the assistant should be helping the participants do the following:
    - Clear the tables of preparation tools and ingredients
    - Stack all tools in the kitchen for cleaning. Optimally there is time and space to have the participants help with clean up.
    - Wipe one table and set it for the class to eat the meal on
    - Wipe a second table if needed and begin to stack the instructor's clean tools and goods for packing
    - Begin washing dishes if time permits

NOTE: For your convenience, Appendix F contains Chef-K kitchen etiquette. Our staff finds it useful to have it printed and mounted in the training area. Review at your convenience with participants or as needed.

After class

- All cooking tools and utensils should be washed, air dried, and put away.
- All perishables should be put away in a refrigerator or sent home.
- All work surfaces should be cleaned, including the sink.
- If class is held in a commercial kitchen, plan on wiping participant fingerprints from refrigerators, stovetops, and cabinets.
- Empty all class waste. Ideally the facility should be able to accommodate separating waste into the following categories:
    - green waste
    - recycled waste
    - trash
- Sweep the floors.

Cleaning supplies and tool list

The instructor will need to provide the following cleaning supplies and kitchen equipment[1]:

- Dish soap
- All-purpose cleaner or anti-bacterial wipes
- Paper towels
- One dish towel per participant per day; the class will use a lot of dish towels. (Plan to launder every day.)

[1] Check with Chef-K management in some cases the youth organization will supply the cleaning supplies and kitchen equipment

- One apron per participant per day (disposable aprons are acceptable)
- One hair net[2] per participant per day (the participants will be given the option of bringing and wearing a baseball style cap from home instead)
- Scouring pad
- Two sponges or dish cloths per day
- Two to four heavy duty oven mitts to use when working with hot pots and pans
- Antibacterial wipes: these are optional but encouraged; they provide an excellent and quick way to clean up between activities during class
- Three to four trivets
- The following consumables:
  - Plastic wrap
  - Zippered plastic bags in sandwich, quart, and gallon sizes for storing leftovers
  - Aluminum Foil
  - Paper towels
  - Napkins
  - Plates
  - Bowls for fruit, etc.
  - Forks, knives, spoons
  - Cups for drinking

After class follow-up

Plan to wash towels, oven mitts, and cloth aprons (unless using disposable aprons) after each class.

Seasonal Variations:

Please note if you are teaching this class during winter, or early spring many of the summer ingredients may not be available. Notes are included for variations and alternative produce and ingredients. Request a Seasonal shopping list.

Note on Desserts:

Fresh fruit is included for each day, however, if there is time and interest, consider "improvising" by making baked apples or bananas in winter, or frozen and pureed bananas in summer. A small bag of whole wheat flour is included in the shopping list to use for this purpose.

[2] Required if working in a certified commercial kitchen

Shopping List for the week

Dinner's Ready -Summer Shopping list

Notes:

- Chef-K recommends 2 separate shopping trips for the week of classes.

  1. Once before camp either Friday or over the weekend for all non-perishable items and produce for Monday and Tuesday.
  2. The second shopping trip is recommended prior to Wednesday class. However, sometimes additional perishable items may need to be purchased later in the week as noted.
  3. Shop once before camp--either Friday or over the weekend—to purchase all non-perishable items, and for the produce that will be used in class on Monday and Tuesday. In order to prevent any chance of spoilage and waste, please do not shop any earlier than 3 days prior to Monday's class.
  4. The second shopping trip is recommended for Tuesday afternoon, or prior to Wednesday's class. If you have any questions concerning items listed in the second round of shopping, feel free discuss them with your Chef-K instructor.

- The day on which the grocery item will be used in class is noted for most items on this list.
- Unless otherwise specified, meat should be fresh, not frozen.
- Nearly all classes require olive oil, fresh garlic, salt, and pepper so plan to always have these on hand.
- The following list is calculated for 1 recipe and the number in parentheses is for 15 participants. Amounts may need to be adjusted when there are more or fewer participants. And remember, older children generally have larger appetites.
- When seasonal foods like tomatoes are not available; canned with low salt added may be used. When other seasonal foods like peaches are not available fresh, buy frozen.

Note: The shopping list reflects the ingredients needed to complete one of each recipe in the menu. Calculate the amount needed for each item in the shopping list on the basis of the expected number of participants. For your convenience, the quantity for 15 participants has been included in parenthesis. For example, item 1 in produce reads:
"1 (2) bunch of baby carrots" – the (2) is the amount needed for 15 participants.

Dinner's Ready

Shopping Day 1 - Summer

Produce

- 1 (2) bunches of carrots Monday ((standard bulk carrots if a bunch is unavailable – about ½ (1) pound)
- 9 (15) zucchini 2(4) Monday, 4(8) Tuesday, 1 (3) Friday
- 4 bunches celery for knife skills, Monday and Wednesday
- 1 (2) basket of cherry tomatoes Monday
- 1 (2) small tomato or ½ (1) basket of cherry tomatoes Wednesday
- Bunches of herbs, such as basil and thyme, 2 bunches parsley (keep refrigerated, with stems in water)
- 4 (8) bunches scallions/green onions for the week
- 8 (12) medium onions for week
- 3 (5) heads garlic for week
- 2 pounds lemons for recipes
- 4 (8) pounds fresh ripe plum tomatoes Wednesday (sometimes called Romano tomatoes)
- 4 (8) bunches fresh basil leaves Wednesday
- 1 red Italian-style torpedo onion, Wednesday (other sweet red onions are ok)
- 2 (4) cups spring greens lettuce mix Wednesday
- 2 (4) pounds green beans Wednesday
- Fresh Fruit throughout the week. **¼ pound per person/per day** (buy what's on sale see the suggestions below)
    - Monday – (3.5 pounds) Assorted Berries are a good choice
    - Tues – (3.5 pounds) Assorted Bananas, cantaloupe, honeydew melon
    - Wed – (3.5 pounds) Assorted plums, peaches, and/or apricots

Canned Goods

- 1 small can tomato paste Tuesday
- 5 (10) cups broth (vegetarian – Low sodium) 4 (8) cups Tuesday, 1 (2) cups Wednesday
- ¼ (1/2) cup of pitted green olives Monday
- 1 (3) 8oz can tomato sauce Friday

Meat or Poultry

- 1 (2) pounds boneless, skinless chicken breasts Monday
- 3(4.5) pounds ground beef (Beef, ground, 85% lean meat / 15% fat, raw) Tuesday
- 2 (3) whole chickens (4-7 pounds each) Mary's or Organic chicken preferred Thursday
- 1/2 (1 ½) pounds ground turkey Friday

Refrigerated / Dairy

- ½ (1) cup of shredded cheddar cheese or other cheese of your choice Monday
- ¾ pound butter Monday
- parmesan cheese for multiple recipes during week
- ¾ (1.5) cup shredded d Monterey jack or cheddar cheese Friday

Grains/Breads/Nuts/Etc.

- 2 (4) cups uncooked brown rice, choose Jasmine or Basmati long grain rice Tuesday
- 4 (8) Tbsp blanched almonds Wednesday
- 1 (2) pounds whole wheat Fusilli or pappardelle or other small dry pasta with "pockets" or ridges (or standard white flour pasta if whole grain is not available)
  Wednesday
- 6 (12) whole wheat tortillas – fajita size (30 g each) or corn tortillas Friday

Oils/Vinegars/Dressings/Condiments

- Large bottle of olive oil (at least 1 quart) – to use every day

Spices / Baking Ingredients

- Kosher salt – every day
- Black Pepper – every day
- dried thyme leaves
- ¼ (1/2) cup whole wheat flour (Consider purchasing this amount from a grocery store that offers bulk ingredients so as not to need to purchase a large quantity. If bulk is unavailable; purchase a 1 pound package.)
- Ground cinnamon
- Ground cumin Friday
- chili powder Friday

Shopping Day 2 – Summer

Produce

- 4 (8) firm but ripe avocados for Friday– if fresh are unavailable purchase from frozen or refrigerator section – do not purchase seasoned guacamole). *Note: be sure to purchase avocados in advance so they will be ripe for Friday.*
- 15 (20) medium-size new potatoes or Yukon gold potatoes Thursday
- 1 bunch Fresh Rosemary Thursday
- (4 pounds) Broccoli, cauliflower, or other seasonal vegetable, ¼ pound per person Thursday
- 1 (2) orange Thursday
- 2 (4) large, firm red- ripe tomatoes Friday
- 1 (2) bunch cilantro, chopped (optional) Friday
- 4 (8) limes for juicing Friday
- 1 (3) yellow summer squash Friday
- 2 (4) ears of fresh corn if fresh is not available purchase 3 cups frozen corn kernels Friday
- 1 (3) mild green chili pepper Friday
- 1 (3) Anaheim or California green chili, seeded Friday
- Fresh Fruit throughout the week. **¼ pound per person/per day** (buy what's on sale or see the suggestions below)
    - Thursday – (3.5 pounds.) Pineapple, bananas, mangos
    - Friday – (3.5 pounds.) watermelon or other melons like cantaloupe and honeydew

Meat or Poultry

- 2 (3) Whole chickens (4-7 pounds each) Mary's or Organic chicken preferred Thursday
- 1/2 (1 ½) pounds ground turkey Friday

Refrigerated / Dairy

- ¾ (1.5) cup shredded Monterey jack or cheddar cheese Friday
- 8 ounces unsalted (preferred) butter Friday optional dessert or coconut oil as an alternative
- ½ cup milk Friday optional dessert
- 4 eggs Friday optional dessert
- 1-quart (1/2 gallon) vanilla ice cream (optional) Friday

Grains/Breads/Nuts/Etc.

- 1 large bag of tortilla chips

Spices / Baking Ingredients

- Ground coriander Friday optional dessert
- Ground cinnamon Friday optional dessert
- Ground cloves) Friday optional dessert
- Small vanilla extract Friday optional dessert
- 2 cups sugar Friday optional dessert
- 1 cup regular or quick-cooking rolled oats Friday optional dessert
- Whole wheat flour – Friday optional dessert

Shopping list – Winter/Early Spring

Notes:

- Chef-K recommends 2 separate shopping trips for the week of classes.

    5. Once before camp either Friday or over the weekend for all non-perishable items and produce for Monday and Tuesday.
    6. The second shopping trip is recommended prior to Wednesday class. However, sometimes additional perishable items may need to be purchased later in the week as noted.
    7. Shop once before camp--either Friday or over the weekend—to purchase all non-perishable items, and for the produce that will be used in class on Monday and Tuesday. In order to prevent any chance of spoilage and waste, please do not shop any earlier than 3 days prior to Monday's class.
    8. The second shopping trip is recommended for Tuesday afternoon, or prior to Wednesday's class. If you have any questions concerning items listed in the second round of shopping, feel free discuss them with your Chef-K instructor.

- The day on which the grocery item will be used in class is noted for most items on this list.
- Unless otherwise specified, meat should be fresh, not frozen.
- Nearly all classes require olive oil, fresh garlic, salt, and pepper so plan to always have these on hand.
- The following list is calculated for 1 recipe and the number in parentheses is for 15 participants. Amounts may need to be adjusted when there are more or fewer participants. And remember, older children generally have larger appetites.
- When seasonal foods like tomatoes are not available; canned with low salt added may be used. When other seasonal foods like peaches are not available fresh, buy frozen.

Note: The shopping list reflects the ingredients needed to complete one of each recipes in the menu. Calculate the amount needed for each item in the shopping list on the basis of the expected number of participants. For your convenience, the quantity for 15 participants has been included in parenthesis. For example, item 1 in produce reads:
"1 (2) bunch of baby carrots" – the (2) is the amount needed for 15 participants.

Shopping Day 1 – Winter / Early Spring

Produce

- 1 (2) bunch of carrots Monday ((standard bulk carrots if a bunch is unavailable – about ½ (1) pound)
- 1 head of red cabbage Monday
- 1 (3) bunches of Swiss chard, Kale, or mixed greens combined, such as collards, or spinach
- 4 bunches celery Monday,
- Bunches of herbs, such as basil and thyme, 2 bunches parsley (keep refrigerated, with stems in water)
- 1 (2) pound white, brown, or Cremini mushrooms
- 4 (6) bunches scallions/green onions for the week
- 8 (12) medium onions for week
- 3 (5) heads garlic for week
- 2 pounds Lemons for recipes
- 1 (3) Oranges Monday
- 1 (2) Apples or pears Wednesday
- 1 Pomegranate (if late fall or Winter and available – you won't find after January)
- 2 pounds fresh ripe plum tomatoes Wednesday (sometimes called Romano tomatoes)
- 1 bunch fresh basil Wednesday, if available
- 1 red Italian-style torpedo onion, Wednesday (other sweet red onions are ok)
- 2 (4) cups spring greens lettuce mix Wednesday
- 2 (4) pound green beans Wednesday if green beans unavailable look for broccoli, or cauliflower
- Fresh Fruit throughout the week. **¼ pound per person/per day** (buy what's on sale see the suggestions below)
    - Monday – (3.5 pounds) apples, or pears, bananas
    - Tues – (3.5 pounds) Bananas, pineapple (if pineapple unavailable – apples or pears)
    - Wed – (3.5 pounds) oranges, kiwi

Canned Goods

- 1 small can tomato paste Tuesday
- 5 (10) cups broth (vegetarian – Low sodium) 4 (8) cups Tuesday, 1 (2) cups Wednesday
- ¼ (1/2) cup of pitted green olives Monday
- 1 (2) 32oz can of low-salt whole tomatoes.
- 1 (3) 8oz can tomato sauce Friday

Meat or Poultry

- 1 (2) pounds boneless, skinless chicken breasts Monday
- 3(4.5) pounds ground beef (Beef, ground, 85% lean meat / 15% fat, raw) Tuesday

Refrigerated / Dairy

- ½ (1) cup shredded cheddar cheese or cheese of your choice Monday
- 1 ½ cups grated parmesan cheese for multiple recipes during week

Grains/Breads/Nuts/Etc.

- 2 (4) cups uncooked brown rice, choose Jasmine or Basmati long grain rice Tuesday
- 4 (8) Tbsp blanched almonds Wednesday
- 1 (2) pounds whole wheat Fusilli or pappardelle or other small dry pasta with "pockets" or ridges (or standard white flour pasta if whole grain is not available)
  Wednesday
- 6 (12) whole wheat tortillas – fajita size (30 g each) or corn tortillas Friday

Oils/Vinegars/Dressings/Condiments

- Large bottle of olive oil (at least 1 quart) – for daily use

Spices / Baking Ingredients

- Kosher salt – every day
- Black Pepper – every day
- dried thyme leaves
- ¼ (1/2) cup whole wheat flour (Consider purchasing this amount from a grocery store that offers bulk ingredients so as not to need to purchase a large quantity. If bulk is unavailable; purchase a 1-pound package.)
- Ground cumin Friday
- chili powder Friday
- ground cinnamon Friday

Shopping Day 2 – Winter / Early Spring

Check with your Chef-K instructor prior to shopping for Thursday and Friday. S/he will advise you on whether the class can make dessert on Friday and if there is enough extra fruit or vegetables to cover the remaining class. If you have opted to have parents join, s/he can guide you on purchasing extra items like tortillas.

Produce

- 4 (8) ripe avocados firm but ripe Avocados for Friday– if fresh are unavailable purchase from frozen or refrigerator section – do not purchase seasoned guacamole). *Note: be sure to purchase avocados in advance so they will be ripe for Friday.*
- 10 (15) medium-size new potatoes or Yukon gold Thursday
- 2 (5) sweet potatoes or yams Thursday
- 1 small butternut squash Friday
- 1 bunch Fresh Rosemary Thursday
- 3 (5 pounds) Broccoli, cauliflower, Brussel sprouts (a combination is good) or other seasonal vegetable, ¼ pound per person Thursday 1/8 pound per person Friday
- 1 (2) orange Thursday
- 2 (4) large, firm red- ripe tomatoes Friday
- 1 (2) bunch cilantro, chopped (optional) Friday
- 4 (8) limes for juicing Friday
- 1 (3) mild green chili Friday
- 1 (3) Anaheim or California green chili, seeded Friday
- 1 ½ pound apples or pears Friday optional dessert
- Fresh Fruit throughout the week. **¼ pound per person/per day** (buy what's on sale or see the suggestions below)
  - Thursday – (3.5 pounds.) pears or apples
  - Friday – (3.5 pounds.) Pineapple, bananas, tangerines

Meat or Poultry

- 2 (3) Whole chicken (4-7 pounds each) Mary's or Organic chicken preferred Thursday
- 1/2 (2) pound ground turkey Friday

Refrigerated / Dairy

- ¾ (1.5) cup shredded Monterey jack or cheddar cheese Friday
- 8 ounces unsalted (preferred) butter Friday optional dessert or coconut oil as an alternative
- ½ cup milk Friday optional dessert
- 4 eggs Friday optional dessert
- 1-quart (1/2 gallon) vanilla ice cream (optional) Friday

Spices / Baking Ingredients

- Ground coriander Friday optional dessert
- Ground cinnamon Friday optional dessert
- Ground cloves Friday optional dessert
- Small bottle Vanilla extract Friday optional dessert
- 2 cups sugar Friday optional dessert
- 1 cup old fashioned Friday optional dessert
- Whole wheat flour – Friday optional dessert

Day 1 Overview for Instructor

Day 1 - Monday

Let's Make a Salad Entrée

Menu

- Seasonal Vegetable Salad with Chicken
- Fresh Fruit

Description

Participants will review basic kitchen safety, kitchen rules for the week. Participants will then learn basic knife skills and prepare the menu.

Objectives

1. Learn basic kitchen practices for the week for safety in the kitchen.
2. Review basic kitchen etiquette for Chef-K classes.
3. Learn basic knife skills.
4. Use knife skills to prepare vegetables for salad.

Lesson setup – Knife Skills

Instructors will provide participants with knives, cutting mats, and vegetables[3]. They will then let the participants practice each of the skills listed in the handout as described in the section below. The instructor will then review each participant's practice knife work: using the table in Appendix I: Knife-Skills Checklist, log the name and results of each participant. Any participant that misses this lesson will not be allowed to use a knife for the remainder of the classes. You will teach participants how to safely handle and use a knife, including an easy way to hold a chef's knife. Participants will learn basic recipe terminology that describes ways to cut up ingredients and will practice cutting with a knife.

It is important to remember that using a knife is a privilege, so instructors should really treat knife usage with special attention. Participants earn the privilege of using a knife by completing the knife safety lesson and following the knife safety guidelines at all times.

[3] Please purchase celery, bell peppers, and onions needed later in the week for Monday's knife skill class.

Knife Safety Quiz Answers

True/False

Directions: respond true or false to following questions:

1) When passing a knife to another person; always present the blade or tip to them. *False*
2) Always make sure a knife is clean and dry before using it. *True*
3) It's a good idea to use the blade to scrape food off of a cutting board. *False*
4) It's best to leave a soiled knife in warm soapy water while you prepare the rest of your meal. *False*
5) Always use a cutting board to protect your counter or table top. *True*
6) If a knife falls it's best to try to catch it before it hits the ground. *False*
7) For the purposes of our kitchen classes, if you are carrying a knife across the kitchen you should call out, "knife coming through." *True*

Multiple choice – select the best answer from a to c

1) A good way to store a knife is:
   a. Lying flat in a drawer with a knife guard.
   b. In a knife block.
   c. *Both a & b are good ways to store knives.*
2) Always keep your knife sharp. The following helps to keep the knife sharp.
   a. Never scrape food off a cutting board with the blade.
   b. Never use a knife for anything except for cutting.
   c. *All of the above.*

Recipe setup

See the game plan in the participant handout. If the carrots are very tender and organic; it is not necessary to peel them. However, if they are standard carrots, have the participants peel them.

Plan to prepare all of the vegetables for the salad today during knife skills. If there is extra celery, it may be saved for later in the week or distributed to the participants to take home after class.

It's best day 1 to have all the participants work as one big unit. As part of knife skills lesson. Then you can have 1 or 2 children make the dressing as you guide them with everyone watching.

Winter Options:

Salad:

Eliminate zucchini, cherry tomatoes, green olives, and pine nuts in the salad. Use ¼ head of red cabbage sliced, 1 orange, peeled, and diced, and either sunflower seeds, or almonds.

Fruit:

Consider apples, bananas, oranges, kiwi since other fruit will be difficult to find.

Clean mats and knives after the knife lesson. Select a group of participants to prepare the fruit selected for today. A good option is an assortment of berries, such as strawberries, blueberries, and raspberries. Have the other participants cut up the poached chicken.

The recipe will be doubled if there are 15 participants.

Consumables needed

- Plates
- Forks
- Knives
- Spoons
- Napkins
- Plastic food wrap

Appliances

- Stovetop or Burner

Tools for class

- Large serving bowl for salad
- Measuring cups and spoons
- Knifes
- Cutting mats
- Large pot with lid to poach chicken
- Wooden spoon

Notes

Day 2 Overview for Instructor

Day 2 - Tuesday

Clean, Separate, Cook, and Chill

Menu: It's not just a Hamburger

- Salisbury Steak with French Onion Sauce
- Rice
- Sautéed Zucchini
- Fresh fruit

Description

You will review food safety and the techniques of sautéing and browning. You will then prepare a Salisbury Steak menu.

Objectives

1. To learn food safety and build on kitchen practices from Day 1.
2. To practice basic knife safety and knife skills.
3. Understand the principle of sautéing
4. Demonstrate the cooking with Salisbury Steak with French Onion Sauce
5. Practice the techniques while preparing the menu for the day.

Lesson setup – Food Safety

This is a fairly straightforward lesson. It works best to try to get a discussion going with the children. The first topic to talk about is their personal cleanliness. The remaining topics make participants aware of safety issues when handling food in everyday situations.

Since the first topic is personal cleanliness, discuss and ensure that each participant knows how to wash his or her hands. It might be useful to use a poster size sheet or a whiteboard as a tool for this class discussion. Have the participants help create a list to cover the topics you will discuss.

Clean

Make sure participants know how to wash their hands. Review the hand-washing instructions in the safety section at the end of the participant handout.

Ask the participants if they know how to clean dishes. See what information they might be able to give you.

Separate

Ask the participants if they've shopped for groceries. Have they bought raw meat? Have they bought vegetables? How do they store them in the basket? Talk about using a cutting board. Ask what order they might prepare food so they don't cross contaminate. Ask whether they think it is okay to place cooked meat on the same plate that the raw meat was on. Ask them about storing raw meat in the refrigerator. Where should they store it, above or below a prepared salad?

Cook

Ask the participants if they have ever cooked meat. Talk about why it is important to cook meat to the correct temperature. Find out if they have any ideas of which foods should be cooked thoroughly. Use the text in the participant handout as an instructor's guide.

Chill

Ask participants what kinds of ingredients they keep in the refrigerator. Talk about why it is important to chill certain ingredients. Use the text in the participant handout as an instructor's guide.

Food Safety Exercise Answers

Directions: Read the paragraph below, and fill in the missing letters for the words with empty spaces.

Whenever I start cooking, I always wash my hands. I always make sure my hair is covered or out of the way. I take off my jacket, roll up my sleeves, and wear an apron to help keep outside germs away from food I am preparing. I always clean countertops and surfaces before preparing food. When I prepare specific food, I always make sure to separate vegetables from raw meats. I always wash fruits and vegetables before beginning. I always chill perishable foods in the refrigerator before and after cooking. I always cook food to the correct temperature to stop any bacteria from growing inside my food.

Recipe setup

It's a good idea to have the children use gloves to handle meat. Also, be very careful to put everything clean and prepared out of the way. Occasionally meat goes flying around the room.

Review the game plan. Plan to have each participant prepare their own "Salisbury Steak". Then have each of them dredge it in the flour. Have them place their finished steaks on a large baking sheet. Remind them of the importance of food safety.

Complete the remaining recipe. When you begin to brown the "steaks", let each participant brown one. Also let them take turns sautéing the onions.

Since it takes a while to have 16 kids brown their patties, place the browned ones in a roasting pan or on a baking sheet in the oven to finish cooking.

NOTE: There is plenty of onion sauce, so you will not need to double the recipe if up to 16 participants. It's ok to prepare the sauce in the pan and also pour on top of the Salisbury steaks in the oven. Let it warm and the flavor build while preparing the rest of the meal.

Winter Options:

If zucchini is not available, use broccoli, Swiss chard, kale, or Brussels sprouts.

Your assistant will need to keep some of the participants outside the kitchen working on the food safety lesson exercise. Remind participants to wash hands again when they come into the kitchen.

Consumables needed

- Bowls
- Spoons
- Paper towels
- Napkins
- Paper plates

Appliances

Stovetop or burner

Tools for class

- Heavy-bottomed pot with lid
- Wooden spoon or heat-proof spoon
- 1-2 Large deep frying pan with lid
- Large baking pan
- Assorted small bowls
- 1 large platter
- 2 Serving bowls
- Plate or pie plate
- Large mixing bowl

- Tongs
- Large serving bowl
- Measuring cups and spoons
- Cutting mats
- Knifes

Day 3 Overview for Instructor

Day 3 - Wednesday

Sum of the Parts

Everyone likes Pasta Menu

- Pasta with seasonal sauce
- Simple Salad
- Italian-Style Green Beans
- Fresh Fruit

Description

Today we will build on Day 1 and Day 2 concepts and begin to understand how to plan daily meals to meet nutritional requirements. Then learn additional basic cooking techniques as we prepare quick and nutritious ways to serve pasta.

Objectives

- Review MyPlate and the food groups
- Learn how to plan a balanced meal
- As a group discuss the case study and as a group complete the menu1 and menu2 comparison
- Prepare our menu
- Enjoy our menu

Background for The Instructor

Most participants will be familiar with MyPlate and the different food groups. Today we will tie the food groups to our daily meals. Food is necessary to help us grow during childhood and teen years and to sustain adults. Food and water keep our body engine running. Eating the correct quantities throughout the day helps us stay healthy. It's important to understand how to eat throughout the day.

Lesson Setup – Sum of the Parts

Materials Setup

Optional Exercise

We have found that by having the participants write down a typical day's menu that it helps them understand the concepts of the food groups learned when reviewing MyPlate. If the participants are middle school age or older this exercise is appropriate.

Case Study

We have found that a very good way to set up this lesson is to use either a poster-sized sticky pad or a white board to outline the key components of the post-test. If you don't have a poster displaying Menu 1 and Menu 2 (poster is available through Chef-K), then write the Menus on the white board or a large sheet of paper. Have extra space to use as you are talking through the lesson.

The ideal approach is to have two colors for the case study poster.

Organizing the Lesson

Plan to talk through the lesson at a very high level. If necessary, review the MyPlate and remind the participants of the basic food groups. The age of the class will determine the amount of time to spend on the lesson. The lesson will have two parts:

1. What's a balanced plate?
2. 10 tips to build a healthy meal (use the USDA Handout DGtipsheet1)

When working with younger children (ages 7 to 10) you can reduce the time reviewing the 10 tips. However, plan to focus a bit more time on the balanced plate portion for younger children. With children ages 11 through high school the time on each part will be reversed, i.e. spend more time on the 10 tips. Consider each piece as you plan the lesson.

Use the blank poster sheet or part of the white board to document what the students are calling out as you talk through each section below:

What's A Balanced Plate?

Go over the three main food categories that make up a healthy plate. These are:

- Protein & Dairy, which include beans, nuts, meat, eggs, milk, and yogurt
- Carbohydrates, which include potatoes, yams, squash, and grains, such as rice, oats, and unrefined starches like whole grain bread or pasta
- Vitamin and mineral-rich foods, which include vegetables and fruit

10 Tips to Build a Healthy Plate

1. Make half your plate veggies and fruit

Vegetables and fruits are full of nutrients and may help to promote good health. Choose red, orange, and dark green vegetables such as tomatoes, sweet potatoes, and broccoli.

2. Add lean protein

Choose protein foods, such as lean beef and pork, or chicken, turkey, beans, or tofu. Twice a week, make seafood the protein on your plate.

3. Include Whole Grains

Aim to make at least half your grains whole grains. Look for the words "100% whole grain" or "100% whole wheat" on the food label. Whole grains provide more nutrients, like fiber, than refined grains.

4. Don't forget the dairy

Pair your meal with a cup of fat-free or low-fat milk. They provide the same amount of calcium and other essential nutrients as whole milk, but less fat and calories. Don't drink milk? Try soymilk (soy beverage) as your beverage or include fat-free or low-fat yogurt in your meal.

5. Avoid extra fat

Using heavy gravies or sauces will add fat and calories to otherwise healthy choices. For example, steamed broccolis are great, but avoid topping it with cheese sauce. Try other options, like a sprinkling of low-fat parmesan cheese or a squeeze of lemon.

6. Take your time

Savor your food. Eat slowly; enjoy the tastes and textures and pay attention to how you feel. Be mindful. Eating very quickly may cause you to eat too much.

7. Use a smaller plate

Use a smaller plate at meals to help with portion control. That way you can finish your entire plate and feel satisfied without over eating.

8. Take control of your food

Eat at home more often so you know exactly what you are eating. If you eat out, check and compare the nutrition information. Choose healthier options such as baked instead of fried.

9. Try new foods

Keep it interesting by picking out new foods you've never tried before, like mango, lentils, or kale. You may find a new favorite! Trade fun and tasty recipes with friends or find them online.

10. Satisfy your sweet tooth in a healthy way

Indulge in naturally sweet dessert dish – fruit! Serve a fresh fruit cocktail or a fruit parfait made with yogurt. For a hot dessert, bake apples and top with cinnamon.

Exercise – Case Study – Post Test

After reviewing the topics for this lesson, have the participants take time to write down a typical meal day if there is time to complete the remaining class.

Then take a few minutes to have two children take a turn at circling the food groups in the case study using the markers. Follow the questions to help guide the participants.
You may have to help them by talking the group through the Case study questions 1 through 8. Have one of the participants take a marker to circle the grains and have another participant use a second marker to circle the information about each of the various food groups. This should help them answer the questions.

At the end of the case study, check the answers and then ask if Menu 1 matches the case study. Point to the case study as you go through it. Do the same for Menu 2. Ask them which menu seems to match the case study.

Case Study Answers

1. Does Menu 1 have a meal that has the three categories of food that make up a healthy plate? yes If so, list the foods below.
    - Protein: turkey
    - Carbohydrate: bread (discuss how this would really be healthy if it was whole wheat or whole grain bread)
    - Vitamin/Mineral-Rich Food: apple
2. How many ounces of the protein group does Menu choice 1 have? 8 oz Does Menu 1 have any lean proteins?
    - No, but you could easily choose lean turkey
3. What category of food is missing for dinner in Menu 1? List a food that would make the dinner balanced.
    - carbohydrate
    - a whole grain, or unrefined starch, any of these could be listed
        - brown rice, barley, couscous, quinoa
        - potatoes, sweet potato, bread, pasta
4. Which meals from Menu 2 have a balanced plate?
    - Lunch
    - After-school snack
    - Dinner

5. What fruit is on Menu 2? What meal could you easily add fruit to?

    - apple
    - breakfast is very easy to have fruit with cereal

6. How many ounces of the grain group does Menu choice 2 have? 6 oz
   What foods in Menu 2 are whole-grains?

    - Whole wheat bread
    - Corn tortilla

7. How many servings are there from the dairy group in Menu 2? 3 servings
   What types of dairy foods should you choose to make a healthy plate?

    - Low-fat dairy products

8. Bonus: According to a sample MyPlate worksheet, a 7-year-old is supposed to have the following foods daily:

   5 oz. of grains
   2cups of vegetables
   1 ½ cups of fruits
   2 1/2 cups of the dairy group
   5 oz. of the protein group

   Looking at the two menu choices, circle the one that meets the MyPlate recommendation for a 7-year-old boy?

   Menu Choice 1 **Menu Choice 2**

Recipe setup

Review the game plan. Have a pot of water boiling before class starts. Consider preparing all of the food prior to the lesson. As the tomato sauce simmers and the pot of water is heating for the pasta would be a good time to do the lesson.

Winter Options:

- 32 oz can of whole tomatoes; low salt may replace fresh tomatoes. Skip to steps 1-5 of the directions.
- It's usually difficult to find fresh basil in non-summer months; so you will have to skip the pesto recipe.
- You can sauté some fresh mushrooms with a clove of minced garlic and parsley to garnish the tomato sauce over pasta.
- Replace tomatoes in salad with either diced apples or pears
- If green beans are not in season, you may be able to use broccoli, Swiss chard, kale, or Brussels sprouts. You may roast vegetables like broccoli, or Brussels sprouts – see recipe Day 4.

Summer & fall – when fresh tomatoes are available:
When preparing the tomato sauce; have each participant practice blanching a tomato. Rinse well in cold water; prior to helping the participants peel, seed, and dice the tomatoes.

Complete the remaining recipes.

Game plan – alternative for instructor's information for Wednesday

If there is not enough oven space for roasted chicken and vegetables on Thursday; plan to prepare the roasted vegetables on Wednesday. Use this game plan:

- Preheat oven 425°
- Heat pot of water for blanching tomatoes
- Prepare salad ingredients
- Prepare roasted vegetable ingredients
- Prepare ingredients for tomato sauce per recipe
- Place vegetables in oven to roast
- Heat pot of water for pasta
- Cook tomato sauce
- Make Green Sauce (summer only)
- Cook pasta
- Assemble salad
- Drain pasta and add red sauce to ½ of cooked pasta

- Add green sauce to other half of the cooked pasta
- Dress Salad
- Serve meal

Consumables needed

- Forks, Spoons
- Paper towels
- Napkins
- Paper plates

Appliances

Stovetop or burner
Oven – if space is limited use the roasted vegetable recipe today from Thursday.

Tools for class

- 5-quart pot
- Wooden spoon or heat-proof spoon
- 1Large deep frying pan with lid
- Large baking pan
- Assorted small bowls
- 1 large platter
- 2 Serving bowls
- Large mixing bowl
- Tongs
- Large serving bowl
- Measuring cups and spoons
- Cutting mats
- Knifes

Day 4 Overview for Instructor

Day 4 - Thursday

Food Allergies

Basic Roasted Meal Menu

- Oven-roasted chicken with potatoes
- Roasted seasonal vegetables
- Fresh Fruit

Description

You will learn about common food allergies, and the causes and symptoms of a food allergy. You will learn the 8 foods that most often cause food allergies.

Objectives

After completing this class, you will be able to:

- Describe what a food allergy is
- Become aware of what to look for on food labels as it pertains to food allergies
- Describe cooking food in the oven

Lesson setup

Today we are talking about food allergies. Discuss who in the class may have an allergy or knows someone with an allergy.

Optional Group Activity

Review ingredient labels on food packaging, using some that you have purchased for class (perhaps the noodles or chicken broth).

Here is an example of an ingredient label for bread:

Whole Wheat Flour, Water, Wheat Gluten, Brown Sugar, Molasses, Soybean Oil, Honey, Yeast, Salt, Cultured Wheat Starch, Oats, Soy Flour, Dough Conditioners

Discuss:

Which ingredients may be a problem for people with food allergies? Which of the 8 foods that most often cause food allergies are in contained in this bread?

Terms for today:

Antibodies	Proteins that are found in blood, used by the immune system to identify foreign objects.
Anaphylactic shock	A very serious allergic reaction that occurs quickly and can cause death.
Casein	A form of milk protein
Epinephrine	A medication for the treatment of anaphylaxis. Once absorbed into the bloodstream, it contracts blood vessels, relaxes airways, relieves cramping in the gastrointestinal tract, decreases swelling, and blocks itching and hives.
Gastrointestinal permeability	Gastrointestinal permeability is sometimes called a "leaky gut" Your gut is part of the immune system and good nutrients pass through the mucosal lining in the gut to the bloodstream. When the lining lets undesirable elements to pass, then it is called a "leaky gut".
Histamine	A chemical that the human body makes, and releases into the blood stream, causing a variety of allergic reactions.

References:

American Dietetic Association Complete Food and Nutrition Guide
Roberta Larson Duyff 2nd Edition 2002

Krause's Food, Nutrition, and Diet Therapy
L. Kathleen Mahan 11th Edition 2004

Community Nutrition for CHAD Majors, Spring 2008
Brown, Boyle, & Hopounden

International Food Information Council (IFIC) Foundation
www.ific.org

Food Allergy and Anaphylaxis Network (FAAN)

Recipe setup

Review the game plan. Have the oven pre-heated when participants arrive. Remind them of issues with food safety when handling raw chicken.

Have the participants wear gloves. Try to encourage them to place garlic on the chicken, rosemary, and salt and pepper. Show them the gizzards, neck and organs. Some children will be curious and want to handle it. Let them explore.

This is another day that it is good to prepare the food and have the chicken roasting prior to beginning the lesson.

Game plan – alternative for instructor's information for Thursday

If there is not enough oven space for roasted chicken and vegetables on Thursday; plan to prepare the green beans from Wednesday on Thursday instead. Use this game plan:

- Preheat oven 425°
- Prepare green bean ingredients, set aside
- Prepare fruit and set aside
- Prepare chicken
- Place chicken & potatoes to roast
- Cook Green beans
- Remove chicken let rest
- Set table then carve chicken and serve
- Clear table
- Enjoy fresh Fruit

Consumables needed

- Bowls
- Forks, Spoons, and knifes
- Paper towels
- Napkins
- Individual cups or small bowls
- Paper plates

Appliances

Stovetop or burner – you will need this if preparing green beans today.
Oven

Tools for class

- 2 roasting pans or 1 roasting pan and a 13- x 9- inch heatproof glass baking dish
- Wooden spoon or heat-proof spoon
- Instant-read style Thermometer
- Ovenproof pan or dish for warming
- 4 or 5 quart pot
- Serving bowls
- Large mixing bowl
- Tongs
- Measuring cups and spoons
- Cutting mats
- Knifes

Day 5 Overview for Instructor

Day 5 - Friday

Celebration

Menu: Celebration Buffet

Mexican Fiesta Menu

- Turkey Tacos
- Shredded Cheese
- Guacamole
- Salsa Fresca
- Tortilla Chips
- Calabacitas with Corn and Tomatoes
- Fresh Fruit

Description

Participants celebrate what they have learned and enjoy a buffet.

Objectives

- Check what the participants have learned by taking quiz
- Participants prepare a celebration buffet
- Have participants and assistant evaluate camp

Lesson setup - Celebration

The last day is a good opportunity to invite parents or other leaders you may wish to include in a "celebration buffet."

There is no formal lesson on Day 5. Have the participants take the 'Check what you've learned' quiz in Participant Handout: Appendix B and handout the evaluation forms to both the assistant and participants. For military camps, please leave behind the Chef-K government information packet.

Recipe setup

A complete menu is planned for Friday. Feel free to use left-over food from earlier in the week so parents can have a sample of other recipes. If oven space is not available heat tortillas wrapped in a towel for 1-2 minute in a microwave.

Winter Options:

In winter, instead of zucchini and yellow squash in the calabacitas recipe; use butternut, or acorn squash. Peel and cube the squash and use it to replace the summer squash. Frozen corn kernels can be used instead of fresh corn.

Calabacitas are simpler to prepare in the oven because they do not take as much hands-on time.

Left-over food from earlier in the week can also be used. If participants are 12 years or older, have them decide on how to reuse the left-overs, otherwise make some suggestions on how food prepared earlier in the week might be presented for a buffet.

Consumables needed

- Paper plates
- Cups
- Forks, spoons, knives
- Napkins or paper towels

Appliances

Blender or food processor
Oven
Stovetop

Tools for class

- Mixing bowls
- Measuring cups and spoons
- Clean cloth or towel
- Large bowl
- Small bowl
- Large spoon
- Heatproof glass baking dish (13- x 9-inches)
- Whisk
- Measuring cups and spoons
- Cutting mats
- Knifes

Appendix A: Northern California Seasonal Vegetables

Farmers' markets and specialty organic grocers have the greatest variety of seasonal vegetables and unique produce, such as green garlic, colorful carrots and radishes, baby carrots, and other baby vegetables. Asian produce markets also have unique local vegetables that are used in Chinese and Southeast Asian cooking.

The availability of vegetables depends on the season and the weather. Generally, vegetables are available for two to three months during a season, although some vegetables have a very short season. Other vegetables are available for more than one season. For simplicity, the following table marks the season during which each vegetable is most commonly found.

Much of the produce throughout the country comes from California, so it is a fairly good gauge of what will likely be available in grocery stores across the United States. To find out what is in season in your area, check with your local farmers' market organization.

Vegetable	**Winter: December, January, February**	**Spring: March, April, May**	**Summer: June, July, August**	**Fall: September, October, November**
Artichokes	√	√		√
Arugula (also called rocket)		√	√	√
Asparagus		√		
Beans, green	√	√	√	√
Beans, fava		√		
Beets	√	√	√	√
Bok choy	√	√		√
Broccoli	√	√	√	√
Brussels sprouts	√			√
Cabbage	√	√	√	√
Carrots	√	√	√	√
Cauliflower	√	√		√

Vegetable	Winter: December, January, February	Spring: March, April, May	Summer: June, July, August	Fall: September, October, November
Celery		√	√	√
Chard (Swiss)	√	√	√	√
Collard greens	√		√	√
Corn			√	√
Cucumbers			√	√
Eggplants			√	
Endive	√	√	√	√
Fennel	√	√	√	√
Garlic	√	√	√	√
Kale	√	√	√	√
Kohlrabi		√	√	
Leeks	√	√	√	√
Lettuce	√	√	√	√
Okra		√	√	
Onions	√	√	√	√
Parsnips	√			√
Peas		√	√	√
Peppers, bell			√	√
Potatoes	√		√	√
Radicchio		√	√	√
Radishes	√	√	√	√
Rhubarb			√	√
Rutabagas	√			√
Scallions (green onions)	√	√	√	√

Vegetable	Winter: December, January, February	Spring: March, April, May	Summer: June, July, August	Fall: September, October, November
Shallots			√	√
Spinach	√	√	√	√
Squash, summer: zucchini, yellow, and others			√	√
Squash, winter: acorn, butternut, and others	√			√
Sweet potatoes				√
Turnips	√			√

Appendix B: Northern California Seasonal Fruit

Farmers' markets and specialty organic grocers have the greatest variety of seasonal fruits and unique produce, such as blood oranges.

The availability of fruit depends on the season and the weather. Generally, fruit is available for two to three months during a season, although some fruits have a very short season. Other fruits are available for more than one season. For simplicity, the following table marks the season during which each fruit is most commonly found.

Much of the produce throughout the country comes from California, so it is a fairly good gauge of what will likely be available in grocery stores across the United States. To find out what is in season in your area, check with your local farmers' market organization.

Vegetable	**Winter: December, January, February**	**Spring: March, April, May**	**Summer: June, July, August**	**Fall: September, October, November**
Apples			√	√
Apricots			√	
Asian pears			√	√
Blackberries			√	√
Blueberries			√	
Boysenberries			√	
Cherries		√	√	
Dates				√
Dried fruits	√	√	√	√
Figs			√	
Grapefruit	√			√
Grapes			√	√
Guavas	√	√		
Kiwifruit	√			√

Kumquats	√			√
Lemons	√	√	√	√
Limes	√			√
Mandarins	√			√
Melons			√	√
Nectarines		√	√	
Oranges	√	√	√	√
Peaches			√	√
Pears	√		√	√
Persimmons	√			√
Plums			√	√
Pluots			√	
Pomegranates				√
Quinces				√
Raspberries			√	√
Strawberries		√	√	
Tangerines	√			√
Tomatoes			√	√

Appendix C: All American: Check what you've learned—with answers

NAME____________________

DATE__________

Answers are in underlined.

Questions:

True/False – respond true or false to the following questions:

1. When passing a knife to another person; always present the blade or tip to them. **(f)**
2. There are 8 common food allergies that we reviewed this week. **(t)**
3. Always make sure a knife is clean and dry before using it. **(t)**
4. It's a good idea to use the blade to scrape food off of a cutting board. **(f)**
5. It's best to leave a soiled knife in warm soapy water while you prepare the rest of your meal. **(f)**
6. Always use a cutting board to protect your counter or table top. **(t)**
7. If a knife falls it's best to try to catch it before it hits the ground. **(f)**
8. Dice and chop are sometimes used interchangeably in recipes. **(t)**
9. Refrigerate or freeze perishables, prepared food, and leftovers within two hours. **(t)**
10. It is important to cook meats, fish, and poultry correctly to ensure that all bacteria are killed. **(t)**

It's a good idea to read food labels; especially if you have food allergies. **(t)**

Multiple choice – select the best answer from a to c

1. A good way to store a knife is:
   a. Lying flat in a drawer with a knife guard
   b. In a knife block
   c. Both a & b are good ways to store knives.

2. Always keep your knife sharp. The following helps to keep the knife sharp.
   a. Never scrape food off a cutting board with the blade.
   b. Never use a knife for anything except for cutting.
   c. All of the above.

3. It is important in food safety to
   a. Plan, Find, Gather, Cook, Serve,
   b. Clean, Separate, Cook, and Chill

4. Which of the following are common food allergens?
   a. Soy
   b. Milk
   c. Peanuts.
   d. All of the above

Fill in the blank for the following questions:

1. Dry heat over 400°F is typically called **roasting**

2. **Dice** refers to food cut into tiny (about 1/8- to 1/4-inch) cubes.

3. USDA recommends you make **half** of your plate fruits and vegetables.

4. **Browning** is a method of cooking that allows a meat or vegetable to become seared quickly over medium heat.

5. **Julienne** refers to foods that have been cut into very thin, matchstick-size strips

6. Can you name the four meals typically eaten throughout the day?

a. **Breakfast**

b. **Lunch**

c. **Snack**

d. **Dinner**

7. If you are a 10-year-old boy or girl, MyPlate recommends you eat 2½ cups of vegetables a day. When would you eat your vegetables?

(any of the following included ok – breakfast, lunch, snack, dinner)

8. What are three types of food you need on a healthy plate?

a. **protein or dairy**

b. **carbohydrates**

c. **vitamin and mineral rich foods; fruits and vegetables**

9. According to USDA how much of your grains should be whole grains?

Half.

10. What type of grains can be part of a healthy plate?

Any response: whole grains, brown rice, whole wheat, oats, buckwheat, quinoa, corn, whole cornmeal, millet, barley, amaranth

11. What are two ways you can reduce the amount of fat you eat?

a. **Substitute whole fat animal products with lean or low-fat animal products**

b. **Choose foods that are naturally low in fat such as grains, beans, vegetables, and fruit**

12. Which of the following are common food allergies?

a. **<u>eggs</u>**
b. **<u>fruit</u>**
c. <u>milk</u>

13. Casein is another name for:

a. wheat
b. <u>milk</u>
c. fish
d. soy

14. Almonds are a type of ____ that many people are allergic to.

a. <u>tree nut</u>
b. soy
c. fish

Appendix D: Web Resources

The following resources are useful for enhancing the Chef-K materials:

- California Foundation for Agriculture in the Classroom: http://www.cfaitc.org.
- Coloring sheets: http://www.fruitsandveggiesmorematters.org/?page_id=78.
- Common food allergens: http://www.foodallergy.org/allergens/index.html.
- CUESA—the Center for Urban Education about Sustainable Agriculture: http://www.ferryplazafarmersmarket.com/markets/.
- Eat a Rainbow: http://www.nutrition.ecsd.net/eat%20a%20rainbow.htm
- Health Benefits of Red Foods, from the Eat a Rainbow series: http://www.thedietchannel.com/Eat-A-Rainbow-Part-1-Health-Benefits-of-Red-Foods.htm. Heidi Reichenberger McIndoo, M.S., R.D. (October 23, 2006).
- Joe's Stuff: www.neworleansschoolofcooking.com.
- Why Is Hand Washing So Important? http://www.kidshealth.org/parent/general/sick/hand_washing.html.

Notes

Appendix E—Overall tool and consumable list

Appliance list

- Stove top or burner
- Electric or stand mixer

Group tool list

Ideally have 1 of each of these items per group of 4 participants

- One set of dry measuring cups
- One set of liquid measuring cups
- One set of measuring spoons
- One can opener
- Butter knives
- Cutting mats (1 for each participant)
- Hand or box grater
- Mixing bowls—large and small
- Large wooden spoon or plastic heatproof spatula
- Whisk

Class tools

- Colander
- Chef's knife
- Paring knife
- Two metal rimmed cookie sheets or large baking pans
- Two 8 or 9" Round cake pans
- Heatproof glass baking dish (13- x 9-inch)
- Large mixing bowls
- 2 Large Stock Pots 10qt or larger
- 2 Large Saucepans 6 qt or larger
- 2 Large skillets or low sided round pots (for sautéing)
- 4 Half-sheet pans
- Large roasting pan with rack
- One 13- x 9- inch heatproof glass baking dish or no-stick baking pan
- Serving platters
- Oven-proof bowl
- Two to four heavy duty oven mitts
- Three to four trivets

- Kitchen shears
- Candy thermometer
- Assorted forks and teaspoons
- Assorted serving forks and spoons

Consumables

- Plastic sleeves to cover recipes for use during class; 1 set per group per class
- Dish soap
- All-purpose cleaner or anti-bacterial wipes (see note below)
- Paper towels (for hand washing and drying, please buy enough for the whole week)
- 1- or 2-oz. tasting cups (plastic recommended)
- One to two dish towels per participant per day
- One apron per participant per day (disposable aprons are acceptable)
- One hair net per participant and assistant per day (participants will be given the option of bringing and wearing a baseball style cap instead of a hairnet)
- Scouring pad
- Two sponges or dish cloths per day
- Plastic wrap
- Zippered plastic bags in sandwich, quart, and gallon sizes for storing leftovers
- Paper or plastic plates
- Forks, knives, and spoons
- Napkins
- Aluminum Foil

NOTE: Antibacterial wipes are optional but encouraged; they provide an excellent and quick way to clean up between activities during class.

Appendix F: Chef-K Kitchen Etiquette

- During all activities, be respectful of the other participants, the instructors, and the assistants.

- Inappropriate behavior is not tolerated at any time in the kitchen. Stoves are hot, and knives are sharp. Please help avoid injuring yourself or others.

- Class starts on time; be considerate of others who arrive on time. No one may join more than 10 minutes after class starts. Our time is limited, and we need time to cook.

- Come to class for the designated amount of time. Be courteous of other participants by not walking in and out of the room. If you have to leave, you are welcome to join us at the next class.

- Do not bring any gum, drinks, or food into the room. Everyone will have an opportunity to share the meal that we prepare.

- Before coming into the room, silence your cell phone.

- When you arrive, remove your jacket, roll up long sleeves, and put long hair in a ponytail. If you are in a commercial kitchen, a hairnet or cap is required. Sign in and wash your hands.

- Wear closed-toed shoes—not sandals or flip-flops.

- Help clean as you go. If you do not have a specific food preparation task, look for something to clean up.

- If you have not tasted something, please request a small taste. Food allergies are the only acceptable reason to avoid tasting. Be respectful if you do not like something that you taste.

- When the meal is ready, please sit and enjoy the food that you have prepared.

- If there are leftovers, you are welcome to take them home. The leftover food will be divided among the participants.

Appendix G: Nutritional Information, Equivalents of Measurements, and Metric Conversion

Nutritional Information

Each Chef-K recipe is accompanied by a table of nutrition facts and just like on any box, jar, or other package these facts represent one serving. Because of variations in ingredients, the values are approximations.

When a recipe gives the quantity of an ingredient as a range, the table provides the nutritional value of the lowest quantity in the range. For example, in a recipe that lists "1-2 ounces sliced Italian prosciutto," the table provides the nutritional value of one ounce of Italian prosciutto.

When a recipe gives more than one option for an ingredient, the table provides the nutritional value of the first option. For example, in a recipe that lists "½ mango or ½ papaya," the table provides the nutritional value of half of a mango.

The nutritional values do not include garnishes or optional ingredients.

Equivalents of Measurements and Metric Conversion

Measure Equivalents

1	Tablespoon	=	3	Teaspoons (tsp)
1	Cup	=	8	Fluid ounces (fl oz)
1	Cup	=	16	Tablespoons (tbsp)
1	Cup	=	48	Teaspoons
1	Pint	=	2	Cups
1	Quart	=	2	Pints
1	Quart	=	4	Cups
1	Quart	=	0.946	Liters
1	Gallon	=	4	Quarts
1	Gallon	=	8	Pints
1	Gallon	=	16	Cups
1	Gallon	=	3.785	Liters
1	Liter	=	1.0267	Quarts

Metric Conversion

1	Ounce	=	28.35	Grams (g)
1	Gram	=	0.0353	Ounces (oz)
1	Gram	=	0.0022	Pounds (lbs)
1	Gram	=	0.001	Kilograms (kg)
1	Pound	=	453.6	Grams
1	Pound	=	16	Ounces
1	Pound	=	0.4536	Kilograms
1	Kilogram	=	1000	Grams
1	Kilogram	=	2.21	Pounds

Appendix H - Chef-K/Noriko's Daily Kitchen Check List

For Guest Chefs / Cooks
Commercial Kitchens

Noriko was a wonderful woman who was in charge of the Vandenberg Air Force Base Youth Kitchen. She helped us develop a guest checklist for the kitchen that served the Air force base youth meals and snacks. Since Chef-K staff and trainers are often guests in a commercial kitchen, we have leveraged Noriko's list and developed a checklist to help ensure any kitchen we use is left ready for inspection. Most commercial kitchens are regularly inspected and must meet health codes at all times. It is a privilege to use the kitchen as a guest; therefore utmost care must be given to maintain our use of any kitchen we use for Chef-K classes. Please leave the kitchen better than you found it. Below is a checklist to help ensure that all of the areas are kept clean.

Date:______________________________

Job	Area	Task	Will /did use it?	Check when done
Setup				
	Participant Prep Tables, Sink & Counter	Wipe Surfaces clean & spray with bleach solution (make fresh daily)		
	Stove & Work Area	Wipe surfaces with sanitizer before starting		
	Oven	Line with foil when roasting meat		
	Workstation – Right of door	Wipe surface with sanitizer before starting		
	Prep Sink & Work Area	Wipe surfaces with sanitizer before starting		
During Prep				
	All Areas	No sitting on counters		
	All Areas	Use cutting mats on work surface when using knifes & sharp tools		
	All Areas	Keep area wiped down between tasks		
Clean up				
	General	Place all leftovers in zip lock bags or bowl with plastic wrap. Use a permanent marker to identify contents & date item.		

Job	Area	Task	Will /did use it?	Check when done
	Dishwashing Station	Set up all dirty dishes in an orderly fashion		
		Dishwashing Machine (chopper) – Turn on & fill (flip down lever on right to fill)		
		Rinse: all dishes, pots & tools of food debris with sprayer		
		Wash Dishes – use trays; do not over load; slide tray into chopper, shut lid; wait until quiet (light will turn off on sanitizer box to the right); remove tray; let air dry When dry, put dishes away – check with kitchen staff if it is ok to leave dishes to air dry until next shift. It is not recommended to dry items with a towel and put away.		
		Dishwashing machine – empty water (flip up lever on the right inside machine to empty); clean out catch basket of any debris; turn off		
		Run garbage disposal with water running		
		Wipe down and sanitize all surfaces in area: sink, counters, edges of all; no water droplets should be noticeable		
	Stove Area	Wipe down all work surfaces & sanitize		
		Stove top – wipe all surfaces; remove any food particles		
	Oven	If used to roast meat, vegetables or bake, look for any dropped or spilled food; wipe up surfaces; clean rack if needed		
	Workstations	Wipe all surfaces & sanitize before leaving		
	Prep Sink	Wipe all surfaces, including sink & sanitize before leaving		
	Refrigerators &	Wipe down any finger prints, etc.		

	Cabinets			
Job	**Area**	**Task**	**Will /did use it?**	**Check when done**
	Hand Washing Station	Wipe down sink & sanitize before leaving		
	Floors	Best to arrange for janitor to follow you – otherwise, remove mats, sweep & mop kitchen floor		
	Garbage	Empty trash buckets & put in new liners		
	Carts	Make sure any carts are back in the kitchen		

Appendix I—Knife Skills Check-off list

Note: Participants must have attended basic knife skill and safety as well as demonstrated specific skills to be listed on this sheet. Only participants on this list will be allowed to use sharp knives in class; others can only use table (butter) knives or plastic knives.

Organization: ____

Date	Participant Name	70% + response to safety questions	Correct Holding Chef Knife	Correct Holding Paring Knife	Demo Julienne	Demo Dicing

Appendix J— Participant Evaluation Form

Participant's Evaluation Form: Dinner's Ready Camp

Date of camp:
Location of camp:

What was your favorite part of the camp?

What was your least favorite part of camp?

What was your favorite ingredient used in the camp?

Name one new cooking term or word that you learned this week:

Was there something that you tasted for the first time? Yes or No

Did you like it? Yes or No

Which recipes would you like to make again?

Would you like to attend another cooking camp in the future?

Appendix K: Participant Handout

Kitchen Primer: Dinner's Ready

Participant Handout

By
Laurie Zerga

For Chef-K®

Kitchen Primer: Dinner's Ready
Participant Handout

2018

For information regarding permissions, contact:

Laurie Zerga, founder
Chef-K
www.chef-k.com

Some portions of this course material have been obtained from public sources or by permission. The following is a list of sources from which this material has been drawn:

- Federal Drug Administration
- National Science Teachers Association (NSTA)
- United States Department of Agriculture (USDA)
- United States Department of Health and Human Services (HHS)

Course: Kitchen Primer: Dinner's Ready Day 1

Day 1 overview

Description

You will learn basic kitchen safety and kitchen rules for the week. You will learn basic knife skills and then prepare a salad menu. This camp is regularly modified to reflect the latest USDA guidelines and recommendations. The Dinner's Ready camp follows the healthiest options using whole grains, flavoring with little salt, as well as no added sugar, and alternatives to butter with natural ingredients such as olive and coconut oil. Dessert throughout the camp is fresh seasonal fruit.

Objectives

1. Learn basic kitchen practices for the week for safety in the kitchen.
2. Review basic kitchen etiquette for Chef-K classes.
3. Learn basic knife skills.
4. Use knife skills to prepare vegetables for salad

Let's Make Salad Entrée Menu

Seasonal Vegetable Salad with Chicken

What will we do today?

- Review the week
- Review basic kitchen safety and kitchen etiquette
- Learn and practice knife skills
- Prepare and enjoy our menu

Camp Overview

This program focuses on simple familiar menus. You will learn to prepare traditional entrees that are tasty and nutritious. As always there is a focus on seasonal ingredients.

By the end of the week, you will have covered basic food preparation, reading recipes, cooking, and cleanup.

The class can accommodate up to 16 students. It provides you with tasting, tactile and hands on experience. Each day includes lesson handouts and recipes for your future reference.

Day/date	Mon	Tues	Wed	Thurs	Fri
Hour 0	Instructor setup	Instructor setup	Instructor setup	Instructor setup	Instructor setup
		Food Safety		Food Allergies	
Hour 1	Intro and Knife Skills	Sauté & Browning Technique	Sum of the Parts	What's in the Oven?	Celebration and certificates
	Let's Make Salad Entrée	It's not just a Hamburger	Everyone likes Pasta	Basic Roasted Meal	Mexican Fiesta Menu
Hour 2	Menu Prep	Menu Prep	Menu Prep	Menu Prep	Prep
	Lunch	Lunch	Lunch	Lunch	Lunch
Hour 3	Cleanup	Cleanup	Cleanup	Cleanup	Cleanup
	Day ends	Day ends	Day ends	Day ends	Day ends
	Instructor cleanup	Instructor cleanup	Instructor cleanup	Instructor cleanup	Instructor cleanup
	Menu	Menu	Menu	Menu	Menu
	Seasonal Vegetable Salad with Chicken	Salisbury steak with French Onion Sauce	Pasta with Red & Green Sauce	Oven Roasted Chicken	Turkey Tacos
	Fresh Fruit	Rice	Simple Salad	Roasted Potatoes & Vegetables	Guacamole & Salsa
		Sautéed Zucchini	Green Beans	Fresh Fruit	Calabacitas (vegetables)
		Fresh Fruit	Fresh Fruit		Fresh Fruit

Staying safe and healthy in the kitchen

Preparing for class

Your safety and health is very important. All participants must follow basic food handling safety procedures during all classes. In addition, you should be very careful when using all appliances, tools, and utensils in the kitchen. Be aware of your safety and the safety of those around you.

Before handling food: rules all participants must follow

- Wash your hands with hot, soapy water. Disposable wipes or hand sanitizer gel are not an alternative unless water is not available.
- Tie back long hair.
- Wear an apron if possible.
- Do not wear jackets.
- Do not wear extra long sleeves that can drag into food; all sleeves must be at least above wrists, and are better at ¾ lengths below elbow.
- Never eat, drink, or chew gum while preparing food. Keep your hands out of your mouth.
- Disinfect all surfaces with a disinfecting bleach solution or appropriate anti-bacterial cleaner.

Student safety

Student safety is important, so be sure to handle food properly.

About safe cleaning and safe disposing of waste

Washing Hands	**Disinfecting**	**Sterilizing tools**	**Safely disposing of material**
Use hot water. Wet hands and add soap. Scrub hands 20 seconds away from the running water. Rinse hands under running water. Dry hands with clean dry towels. Only if water is not available, use disposable wipes or hand sanitizer gel.	Make a bleach solution: 20 ml of bleach with 1 liter tap water. If bleach is not available, use antibacterial cleaner. Wipe counter of all visible soil. Spray all work surfaces and leave on for 2 minutes. Note: bleach solution loses effectiveness within 24 hours.	Wash all kitchen tools and utensils. If possible, use a dishwasher that has been tested for the correct temperature. If an appropriate dishwasher is not available, wash with hot soapy water and rinse.	Dispose of raw meat scraps by placing in a sturdy plastic bag. Seal and dispose of the bag. Recycle paper, glass jars, cans, and milk cartons. Place vegetable and fruit waste in the "green bin".

Using appliances, tools and utensils

- Be respectful of the heat. Stoves, pots and pans, as well as oil and water will get hot. Use appropriate oven mitts, hot pads, and trivets to protect yourself and counter tops.
- Knives and forks are sharp. Follow safety instructions to avoid cutting yourself or those near you.
- Electric appliances often have safety features, but participants should still be alert at all times when using them.

All participants must be respectful of their classmates during class. Inappropriate behavior will not be tolerated at any time in the kitchen.

Chef-K Kitchen Etiquette

- During all activities, be respectful of the other participants, the instructors, and the assistants.
- Inappropriate behavior is not tolerated at any time in the kitchen. Stoves are hot, and knives are sharp. Please help avoid injuring yourself or others.
- Class starts on time; be considerate of others who arrive on time. No one may join more than 10 minutes after class starts. Our time is limited, and we need time to cook.
- Come to class for the designated amount of time. Be courteous of other participants by not walking in and out of the room. If you have to leave, you are welcome to join us at the next class.
- Do not bring any gum, drinks, or food into the room. Everyone will have an opportunity to share the meal that we prepare.
- Before coming into the room, silence your cell phone.
- When you arrive, remove your jacket, roll up long sleeves, and put long hair in a ponytail. If you are in a commercial kitchen, a hairnet or cap is required. Sign in and wash your hands.
- Wear closed-toed shoes—not sandals or flip-flops.
- Help clean as you go. If you do not have a specific food preparation task, look for something to clean up.
- If you have not tasted something, please request a small taste. Food allergies are the only acceptable reason to avoid tasting. Be respectful if you do not like something that you taste.
- When the meal is ready, please sit and enjoy the food that you have prepared.
- If there are leftovers, you are welcome to take them home. The leftover food will be divided among the participants.

Knife Safety

A knife is one of the most important tools used in the kitchen. It is used to dice, julienne, mince, and slice food.

Important: Knives should be cared for properly and kept sharp. If not used carefully and with proper respect, they can cause serious injury.

Type of knife	Uses
Chef's knife	For preparing many kinds of ingredients. Usually the largest knife in the kitchen, a chef's knife has a wide blade that is 8 to 10 inches long. It is one of the most commonly used knives.
Paring knife	For peeling and coring fruits and vegetables, cutting small ingredients, and slicing. A paring knife's blade is 2½ to 4 inches long. It is one of the most commonly used knives.
Boning knife	For boning meat and trimming fat before cooking. A boning knife blade is 4 to 5 inches long and is flexible so that it can curve around meat and bone.
Bread knife	For slicing bread. A bread knife blade is 6 to 10 inches long and is serrated. When using a serrated knife, use a sawing motion. Most experts recommend a serrated knife that has pointed serrations, instead of wavy serrations, for better control and longer knife life.
Carving knife	For cutting cooked meat—for example, for carving a roast beef or a whole roasted chicken. A carving knife's blade is 10 to 12 inches long and is flexible to make it easier to cut off meat around bones.
Utility knife	For slicing meat and cheese. A utility knife is longer than a paring knife but smaller than a chef's knife. Its blade is 5 to 8 inches long. It is also called a sandwich knife.

Tips for Handling Knives Safely…use same edit notes from Brunch All Day

- Always pass a knife to another person with the handle toward the other person. The person taking the knife is presented with the handle rather than the blade or tip.
- Never run or cause a distraction while someone is using a knife in the same room.
- Keep knives clean and dry. A wet knife can slip out of your hand.
- Always keep knives sharp. Never use a knife's blade to scrape food off a cutting board because it dulls the knife. Never use a knife for anything but cutting food.

- Always use a cutting board to protect countertops. Consider putting damp paper towels or tacky shelf liner under the cutting board to prevent slippage.
- Always lay down knives with the blade flat. Do not put a knife down on the flat or sharp edge of the blade.
- *Never* try to catch a falling knife. Let the knife fall to the floor and then pick it up. It's safer to wear shoes while cooking so that a falling knife cannot cut your foot.
- Always wash a knife in warm, soapy water, with the blade away from you. Dry the knife and store it in a knife block or flat in a drawer. If you store a knife in a drawer, cover the blade with a knife guard, which is available at kitchen stores.
- Never leave a knife in a pan of soapy water. You could accidentally grab the knife by the blade and cut yourself.
- When walking through class with a knife, hold the knife beside your leg with the point down and call out, "knife coming through".

How to Hold a Knife

You will have an opportunity to try cutting different items throughout the week.

Always use your dominant (right or left) hand to hold a knife handle and use the other hand as a helper.

Note: For simplicity, the instructions and photographs in this procedure use a right-handed person as an example.

Claw and Dagger

1. Grasp the knife handle with your dominant (right or left) hand.
2. Curl the fingers of your other hand into a claw shape, and put your knuckles flat against the dull edge of the blade, keeping your fingers away from the sharp edge.

Figure 1: Holding a knife – claw and dagger

Note: For people with small hands, it is often easier to carefully hold the dull edge of the blade with the thumb and index finger while the other fingers grasp the knife's handle. This technique gives small hands more control over the knife.

Your helper hand—the "claw" hand—is at greatest risk of an accidental cut. However, when your hand is in a claw, your fingertips will not get cut.

Bridge

Sometimes, something you are cutting is too small to comfortably hold it with your claw. In this case you can use a bridge position for your helper hand.

1. Grasp the knife handle with your dominant (right or left) hand.
2. Place your thumb and pointer finger of your helper hand into an arch form. Then hold the food with thumb and finger. Take the knife and fit it between the arch or bridge of your hand and carefully, cut down the center of the food item.

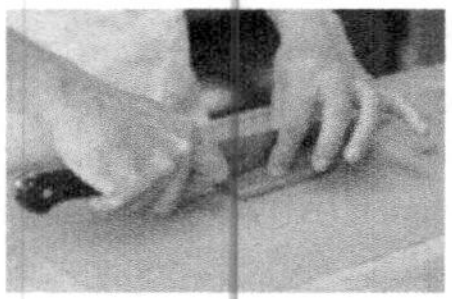

Figure 2 – Holding a knife – bridge

Power Push – flat hand

Other times, when you are mincing herbs, or perhaps a food item is a bit hard to cut, you will need to put a bit of power into the knife. You can place your tip on the cutting board, start the cut and then place your helper hand on top of the knife with a flat hand. Use your body weight to push down.

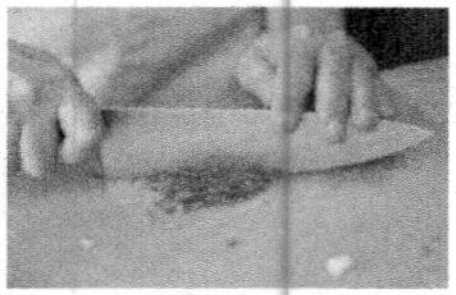

Figure 3: Holding a knife – Power push

Cutting Fruits and Vegetables

If you are right-handed, hold the knife handle with your right hand and curl your left hand into a claw.

If you are left-handed, hold the knife handle with your left hand and curl your right hand into a claw. Put your "claw" hand on the food, with your fingers curled, and use your knuckles as a guide.

Figure 2: Curl your fingers and use your knuckles as a guide

Dicing, Chopping, or Mincing

Uncurl your "claw" hand and rest your fingers on the knife's dull edge.

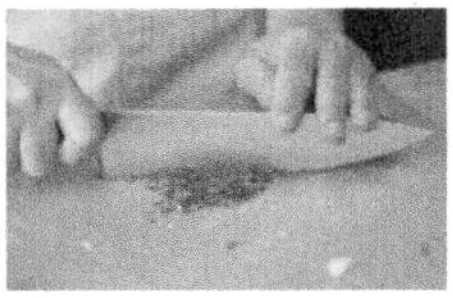

Figure 3: Fingers on top (dull edge) of the knife

Knife Terminology

The recipes in this course use the following terms to refer to ways of cutting ingredients.

Term	**What it means**	**Example**
Chop	To cut into rough pieces. You can chop coarsely (into big pieces) or finely (into small pieces). Recipes often say *coarsely chop* or *finely chop*…	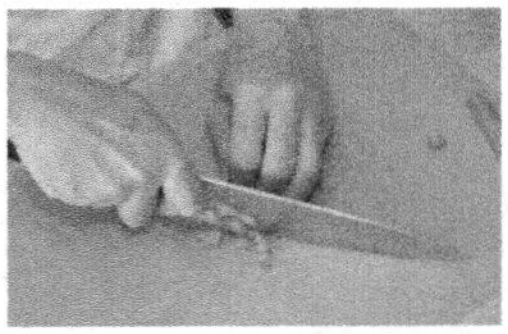
Dice	To cut food into tiny (about ⅛-inch to ¼-inch) cubes	
Julienne	To cut into very thin (matchstick-size) strips a. Cut the food into slices that are ⅛ inch thick. b. Stack the slices and cut them into strips that are ⅛ inch thick. c. Cut the strips to the desired length	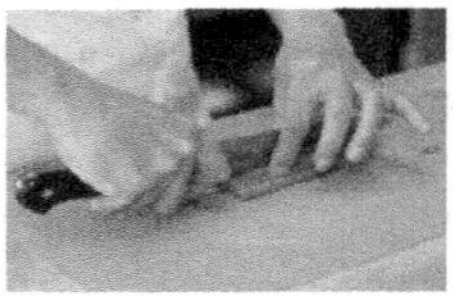
Mince	To chop into very small pieces (smaller than when chopped).	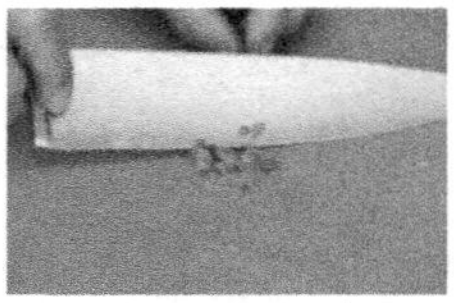
Slice	To cut with a knife.	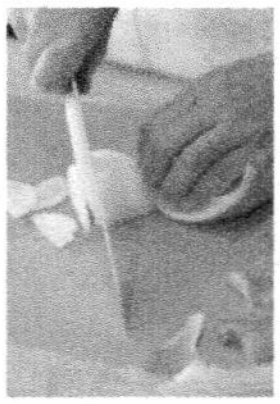

Practice Using a Knife

Important: Carelessness or failure to follow the knife safety guidelines described in this class will result in a loss of the knife privileges. You will not be allowed to use a knife in class.

Practice holding a knife and cutting ingredients. After some practice, your instructor will confirm that you are doing it correctly. Once your instructor has confirmed that you can do the following knife tasks, you can use a knife in all Chef-K classes.

- Demonstrate how to hold a chef's knife.
- Julienne a carrot and a stalk of celery.
- Dice a carrot and a stalk of celery.
- Mince an herb.
- Peel and slice an onion.
- Demonstrate how to hold a paring knife.

Your instructor will log the results of your knife practice in the knife skills checklist.

Knife Safety Quiz

True/False

Directions: respond true or false to following questions:

1) When passing a knife to another person; always present the blade or tip to them.
2) Always make sure a knife is clean and dry before using it.
3) It's a good idea to use the blade to scrape food off of a cutting board.
4) It's best to leave a soiled knife in warm soapy water while you prepare the rest of your meal.
5) Always use a cutting board to protect your counter or table top.
6) If a knife falls it's best to try to catch it before it hits the ground.
7) For the purposes of our kitchen classes, if you are carrying a knife across the kitchen you should call out, "knife coming through."

Multiple choice – select the best answer from a to c

1) A good way to store a knife is:
   a. Laying flat in a drawer with a knife guard.
   b. In a knife block.
   c. Both a & b are good ways to store knives.
2) Always keep your knife sharp. The following helps to keep the knife sharp.
   a. Never scrape food off a cutting board with the blade.
   b. Never use a knife for anything except for cutting.
   c. All of the above.

Day 1: Let's Cook

Let's Make a Salad Entrée

Menu

Seasonal Vegetable Salad with Chicken
Fresh Fruit

Game plan

1. Prepare vegetable salad ingredients – reserve ends & scraps for poaching chicken
2. Poach chicken & let cool
3. Prepare the fruit
4. Assemble salad add sliced chicken and dress
5. Set the table and set out drinks.
6. Enjoy meal
7. Clear table.
8. Serve fresh fruit

Recipe: Simple Poached Chicken

Serves 8-10

Sometimes when you are preparing multiple recipes you have onion skins, pieces of extra carrots, or other vegetables. These are good to save and add to the poaching liquid to add flavor.

Ingredients

- 1-pound boneless, skinless chicken breast
- Vegetable ends and scraps (optional)
  Example: onion skin & root, ends of carrots
- Salt and pepper (1/8 tsp each or to taste)
- Water to cover

Directions

1. Place chicken breasts in a large pot
2. Add vegetable scraps if you are using them.
3. Season with salt and pepper
4. Add enough water to cover chicken by 1-inch
5. Bring to boil
6. Reduce heat and let simmer 20 minutes. Remove from heat and let cool to room temperature. Refrigerate until ready to slice for salad.

Recipe: Seasonal Vegetable Salad with Chicken

Serves 8

This is a wonderful salad created from whatever is in season. In early summer, you might find dainty bunches of carrots, new celery, tomatoes and early zucchini. Add an assortment of herbs and you'll have a wonderful crunchy salad. The chicken, cheese and toasted nuts mean it can be a meal in itself. Below finds an example of vegetables; but feel free to try others.

Ingredients

- 1 bunch of baby carrots diced (standard bulk carrots may be used if baby carrots are unavailable – about ½ pound)
- 2 zucchinis diced
- 2 ribs celery diced
- 1 basket of cherry tomatoes halved
- ¼ cup of pitted green olives
- ½ cup of shredded cheddar cheese of your choice
- ¼ cup of toasted pine nuts—or sunflower seeds or almonds
- 1pound poached boneless, skinless chicken breasts cut into slices
- Assorted fresh herbs, such as basil, thyme, parsley torn into pieces
- ¼ cup olive oil
- ¼ cup fresh lemon juice
- Salt & pepper to taste

Directions

1. Prepare all vegetables as described above. If the carrots are very tender and organic; it is not necessary to peel them. However, if they are standard carrots, have the participants peel them.
2. Combine vegetables, olives, cheese, nuts and herbs into a bowl
3. Gently toss with olive oil
4. Add lemon juice and salt and pepper.

Winter Option:

Eliminate zucchini, cherry tomatoes, green olives, and pine nuts
Use ¼ head of red cabbage sliced, 1 orange, peeled, and diced, and either sunflower seeds, or almonds.

Nutritional Values

Nutrient Name	Nutrient Value	Unit
Calories	290	
Total Fat	21	g
Saturated Fat	4	g
Trans Fat	0	g
Cholesterol	50	mg
Sodium	220	mg
Carbohydrates	7	g
Dietary Fiber	2	g
Sugars	3	g
Protein	20	g
Vitamin A		IU
Vitamin C		mg
Calcium		mg
Iron		mg

This dish qualifies for USDA low sodium dish.

Fresh Fruit

Serves 4

Ingredients

- ¼ pound fruit per person

Directions

1. Wash, dry, and slice fruit onto a platter for serving.

Sample fruit combinations:

- Assorted berries like strawberries, blueberries, raspberries, and blackberries.
- Melon, like cantaloupe, and honey dew
- Exotic fruit, like mango, pineapple, and bananas
- Stone fruit, like plums, nectarines, peaches, and apricots.
- Fall fruit, like apples, bananas, and pears.
- Winter fruit, like bananas, oranges, nectarines, and kiwi.

Nutrition varies by type of fruit.

Course: Kitchen Primer: Dinner's Ready Day 2

Day 2 overview

Description

You will review food safety and the techniques of sautéing and browning.
You will then prepare a Salisbury steak menu.

Objectives

1. Learn food safety and build on kitchen practices from Day 1.
2. Practice basic knife safety and knife skills.
3. Understand the principle of sautéing and browning
4. Demonstrate the cooking with Salisbury steak with French onion sauce
5. Practice the techniques while preparing the menu for the day.

It's not just a Hamburger Menu

Salisbury steak with French Onion Sauce
Rice
Sautéed Zucchini
Fresh fruit

What will we do today?

- Review basic knife safety and knife skills
- Review basic food safety
- Discuss Sauté and Browning Technique
- Prepare Salisbury Steak menu
- Practice knife skills while preparing our menu
- Enjoy our menu

Clean, Separate, Cook, and Chill

Food safety is the most important factor in cooking. It doesn't matter how delicious or complicated your recipe is; if the food makes people sick because of improper cooking or handling, all your efforts will be wasted. You can't always tell if a food is safe to eat by how it looks or tastes. Proper storage, cooking, and handling are the only ways to ensure safe food.

Safe steps in food handling, cooking, and storage are essential to prevent food-borne illness. You can't see, smell, or taste harmful bacteria that may cause illness.

The United States Department of Agriculture (USDA) uses four simple words to help you remember food safety rules, and we'll learn one more. They are **clean**, **separate**, **cook**, and **chill**. Let's learn about each term.

- **Clean —** Wash hands and surfaces often.
- **Separate** — Don't cross-contaminate.
- **Cook —** Cook to proper temperatures.
- **Chill —** Refrigerate promptly.
- **Caution** — Be cautious around heat and sharp tools.

Clean

It is important to keep your hands and all surfaces clean before, during, and after handling food.

Separate

Cross-contamination is the scientific word that describes the process of bacteria spreading from one food product to another. There is a high risk of this happening when people handle raw meat, poultry, and seafood, so keep these foods and their juices away from ready-to-eat and other raw foods such as produce.

It's really important to ensure that you do not introduce bacteria from raw meats, fish, and poultry to raw produce. This means you should always make sure to thoroughly clean your work area after handling different types of ingredients. This helps ensure that you don't cross-contaminate your ingredients.

- Separate raw meat, poultry, and seafood from other foods in your grocery shopping cart and in your refrigerator.
- If possible, use a different cutting board for raw meat products than you use for preparing produce and other foods.
- Always wash hands, cutting boards, dishes, and utensils with hot soapy water after they come in contact with raw meat, poultry, and seafood.
- Make sure to wash and disinfect your work area after preparing raw meat, fish, or poultry, and before handling other raw or cooked foods(for example, lettuce and tomatoes for salad).
- Never place cooked food on a plate which previously held raw meat, poultry, or seafood.

There are several places besides your work area where you have to be careful to avoid cross contamination. Here are some examples:

- When shopping, don't put raw produce, vegetables, and lettuces near raw meat in your shopping cart.
- Cooked food, packaged foods, and produce should always be placed on higher refrigerator shelves than raw meats, fish and poultry. Separating food this way ensures that any drippings from meat, fish or poultry don't contaminate the other foods.

Cook

Always cook food to the correct temperatures. It is particularly important to cook meats, fish, and poultry correctly to ensure that all bacteria are killed. Food safety experts agree that foods are properly cooked when they are heated for a long enough time and at a high enough temperature to kill the harmful bacteria that cause food-borne illness.

- Use a clean thermometer, which measures the internal temperature of cooked foods, to make sure meat, poultry, casseroles, and other foods are cooked all the way through.
- Cook roasts and steaks to at least 145°F. Whole poultry should be cooked to 180°F for doneness.
- Cook ground beef to at least 160°F. Information from the Centers for Disease Control and Prevention (CDC) link eating undercooked, pink ground beef with a higher risk of illness. If a meat thermometer is not available, do not eat ground beef that is still pink inside.
- Cook eggs until the yolk and white are firm. Don't use recipes in which eggs remain raw or only partially cooked.
- Fish should be cooked until opaque and/or flakes easily with a fork.

Chill

Refrigerate foods quickly because cold temperatures keep harmful bacteria from growing and multiplying. Make sure to set your refrigerator no higher than 40°F and the freezer unit at 0°F. Check these temperatures occasionally with an appliance thermometer. Then fight bacteria (Fight BAC!™) by following these steps:

- Refrigerate or freeze perishables, prepared foods, and leftovers within two hours.
- Never defrost food at room temperature. Thaw food in the refrigerator, under cold running water, or in the microwave. Marinate foods in the refrigerator.
- Divide large amounts of leftovers into small, shallow containers for quick cooling in the refrigerator.
- Don't pack the refrigerator. Cool air must circulate to keep food safe.

Shopping Tips

- Purchase refrigerated or frozen items after selecting your non-perishables.
- Never choose meat or poultry in packaging that is torn or leaking.
- Do not buy food past "Sell-By," "Use-By," or other expiration dates.
- Put raw meat and poultry into a plastic bag so meat juices will not cross-contaminate ready-to-eat food or food that is eaten raw, such as vegetables or fruit.
- Plan to drive directly home from the grocery store. You may want to take a cooler with ice for the perishables.

Food Safety Exercise

Directions: Read the paragraph below, and fill in the missing letters for the words with empty spaces.

Whenever I start cooking, I always wash my **h** _ _ _ _. I always make sure my **h** _ _ _ is covered or out of the way. I take off my jacket, roll up my sleeves, and wear an **a** _ _ _ _ to help keep outside germs away from food I am preparing. I always **c** _ _ _ _ countertops and surfaces before preparing food. When I prepare specific food, I always make sure to **s** _ _ _ _ _ _ _ vegetables from raw meats. I always **w** _ _ _ fruits and vegetables before beginning. I always **c** _ _ _ _ perishable foods in the refrigerator before and after cooking. I always **c** _ _ _ food to the correct temperature to stop any bacteria from growing inside my food.

SEPARATE

DON'T CROSS-CONTAMINATE

Cross-contamination (*kros \ken-tamé-ná shen*) is the scientific word for how bacteria are spread from one food product to another. This is especially true when handling raw meat, poultry and seafood, so keep these foods and their juices away from ready-to-eat foods!

CAN YOU FIND THE FOOD HANDLING MISTAKES?

Just another typical day in an average household where many mistakes can be made when handling food! Circle all the mistakes, and learn to be a safe food handler! (The answers can be found by reading "Here's How to Fight BAC!™")

Here's How To Fight BAC!™

- **Separate** raw meat, poultry and seafood from other foods in your grocery shopping cart and in your refrigerator.
- **If possible,** use a different cutting board for raw meat products.
- **Always** wash hands, cutting boards, dishes and utensils with hot, soapy water after they come in contact with raw meat, poultry and seafood.
- **Never** place cooked food on a plate which previously held raw meat, poultry and seafood.

WORD SEARCH

C	Y	S	S	C	I	E	N	C	E	E	E	E
O	R	D	S	O	A	P	Y	R	C	N	T	Q
I	W	I	C	O	H	Q	B	O	L	C	A	T
E	A	S	U	S	I	C	K	S	E	E	R	T
H	S	I	T	W	E	T	C	S	A	R	A	R
D	H	N	T	K	C	E	O	C	N	O	P	E
U	H	F	I	G	H	T	U	O	P	S	E	T
T	A	E	N	G	B	T	N	N	L	S	S	A
A	N	C	G	E	A	F	T	T	A	E	P	W
E	D	T	B	G	C	P	E	A	T	A	Y	T
M	S	S	O	T	T	O	R	M	E	F	Y	O
W	A	A	A	S	E	U	S	I	E	O	D	H
A	D	F	R	S	R	L	E	N	I	O	A	Y
R	O	E	D	C	I	T	R	A	S	D	S	X
R	L	R	O	F	A	G	H	T	C	I	M	R
Y	R	T	L	U	O	P	C	E	I	E	T	L

WORD BANK:
RAW MEAT
WASH HANDS
CROSS CONTAMINATE
CLEAN PLATE
CUTTING BOARD
DISINFECT
SEPARATE
FIGHT
BACTERIA
POULTRY
COUNTERS
SCIENCE
SAFE
SEAFOOD
SOAPY
HOT WATER
SICK

REMEMBER...
WASH YOUR HANDS WITH HOT, SOAPY WATER BEFORE HANDLING FOOD!

U.S. DEPARTMENT OF AGRICULTURE

Sauté and browning technique

What is sautéing?

One technique for cooking is called "sautéing". Sauté is a French word, and the literal translation in French is "to jump" (from the verb, sauter). When sautéing items; chefs will "toss" the food in a pan in such a way that its contents fly through the air, turn over and fall back into the pan. The food is cooked quickly in a small amount of oil or other fat in a skillet or sauté pan over direct heat.

How to sauté

- Before you begin to sauté, it is important to have everything prepared and located near the stove.
- Put the pan on the burner and turn burner to medium high heat. Allow the pan to heat; it should not be cold when you add oil or food to it.
- When the skillet is hot, add enough oil to thinly coat the bottom of the pan. Too little oil may make food cook unevenly and stick to the pan.
- When the oil is hot, add the food carefully to the pan.
- You're Sautéing!

What is browning?

Another technique is called "browning". Browning is a cooking technique that allows a meat or vegetable to become seared quickly over medium high heat. Usually it gets brown marks from the heat of the pan. Typically, after browning liquid is added to the pan to bring up flavors from the bits attached to the pan. The ingredient is then simmered slowly to finish cooking.

Day 2: Let's Cook

It's not just a Hamburger

Menu

Salisbury steak with French Onion Sauce
Rice
Sautéed Zucchini
Fresh fruit

Game plan

1. Prepare vegetables for each recipe and set aside
2. Prepare the fresh fruit and refrigerate or leave out at room temperature.
3. Begin cooking rice.
4. Follow Salisbury steak recipe.
5. Make the onion sauce in the skillet used for Salisbury steak recipe. The meat drippings flavor the sauce.
6. Keep steak in a warm 325° oven while preparing the remainder of the meal.
7. Sauté zucchini when sauce is almost done simmering.
8. When rice and zucchini are done, remove from heat & place in serving bowl
9. Set the table
10. Enjoy meal
11. Serve fresh fruit
12. Clear table
13. Clean up

Recipe

Salisbury steak with French Onion Sauce

Serves 12

Ingredients Salisbury Steak

Steaks:

- 3-pound ground beef (Beef, ground, 85% lean meat / 15% fat, raw)
- ½ cup fresh parsley chopped
- 6 Tbsp scallions finely chopped
- 2 tsp salt
- ½ tsp black pepper
- 2 Tbsp whole wheat flour
- 1 Tbsp olive oil

Optional garnish: parmesan cheese

Directions

1. Preheat oven to 325° oven
2. Combine meat, parsley, scallions, salt & pepper
3. Divide evenly into 12 portions and shape into patties ¾- to 1-inch thick patties.
4. Place flour in shallow bowl or plate and dredge each patty in flour
5. Heat oil in large pan over medium-high heat.
6. Add patties and sauté 3 minutes each side, until browned
7. Remove from pans and place in a roasting pan. Keep warm in the oven while preparing the rest of the dish.
8. Reserve pan for preparing Onion Sauce. (Do not wash!)

Ingredients – Onion Sauce

Sauce:

- 4 medium onions sliced
- 4 garlic cloves minced
- 3 Tbsp tomato paste
- 2 Tbsp whole wheat flour
- 4 cups broth (beef or vegetarian – Low sodium)
- 1 tsp salt
- 1 tsp dried thyme leaves or1 tablespoon chopped fresh thyme leaves

Directions

1. Add onions to pan; sauté 5 minutes
2. Stir in garlic and tomato paste; sauté 1 minute more
3. Sprinkle with excess flour into pan, sauté 1 minute more
4. Whisk in broth, salt and thyme
5. Return meat to pan and bring broth to a boil
6. Reduce heat to medium and cover. Simmer 10 minutes.
7. Place a steak and spoonful of onion sauce on plate
8. Garnish with parsley & parmesan (optional)
9. Repeat for remaining servings.

Nutritional Values

Nutrient name	Nutrient value	Unit
Calories	290	
Total Fat	18	g
Saturated Fat	7	g
Trans Fat	1	g
Cholesterol	75	mg
Sodium	720	mg
Carbohydrates	7	g
Dietary Fiber	1	g
Sugars	3	g
Protein	24	g
Vitamin A	--	IU
Vitamin C	--	mg
Calcium	--	mg
Iron	--	mg

This dish qualifies for USDA Low calories with a portion size of 290g and meals and main dishes of 120 calories or less per 100g.

Recipe

Basic Rice

Serves 8

Ingredients

- 2 cups uncooked rice choose Jasmine or Basmati long grain rice (or try brown rice)
- 4 cups water
- ¼ tsp salt

Directions

1. Place water and salt in a 2-quart pot, cover and bring to boil over high heat
2. When water is boiling, add rice, stir, cover pot and reduce heat to low
3. Cook for 20 minutes

Note: Do not peek at rice; leave it covered so steam will not escape from the pot..

Nutritional Values for white rice

Nutrient name	Nutrient value	Unit
Calories	170	
Total Fat	0	g
Saturated Fat	0	g
Trans Fat	0	g
Cholesterol	0	mg
Sodium	55	mg
Carbohydrates	37	g
Dietary Fiber	< 1	g
Sugars	0	g
Protein	3	g
Vitamin A	--	IU
Vitamin C	--	mg
Calcium	--	mg
Iron	--	mg

Nutritional Values for brown rice

Nutrient name	Nutrient value	Unit
Calories	170	
Total Fat	0	g
Saturated Fat	0	g
Trans Fat	0	g
Cholesterol	0	mg
Sodium	75	mg
Carbohydrates	36	g
Dietary Fiber	2	g
Sugars	0	g
Protein	4	g
Vitamin A	--	IU
Vitamin C	--	mg
Calcium	--	mg
Iron	--	mg

% Daily Values are based on a 2000 calorie diet

Using brown rice for this dish qualifies for USDA low total fat, saturated fat free, cholesterol free, and sugar free.

Sautéed Zucchini

Serves 4

Ingredients

- 2 medium zucchinis
- 1 Tbsp olive oil
- 1 garlic clove coarsely chopped
- 1/8 tsp salt and pepper or to taste

Directions

1. Wash and dry zucchini
2. Quarter zucchini and slice the quarters into 1-inch pieces
3. Heat a 10- to 12-inch sauté pan over medium-high heat.
4. Add olive oil
5. Add zucchini and sauté for 3-4 minutes until softened but not mushy.
6. Add garlic and sauté 1-2 minutes longer.
7. Season with salt and pepper to taste and serve immediately.

Nutritional Values

Nutrient name	Nutrient value	Unit
Calories	45	
Total Fat	3.5	g
Saturated Fat	0.5	g
Trans Fat	0	g
Cholesterol	0	mg
Sodium	50	mg
Carbohydrates	4	g
Dietary Fiber	1	g
Sugars	2	g
Protein	1	g
Vitamin A	--	IU
Vitamin C	--	mg
Calcium	--	mg
Iron	--	mg

This dish qualifies for USDA low calories, total saturated fat, cholesterol free, and low sodium.

Winter Options:

If zucchini is not in season, you may be able to use broccoli, Swiss chard, kale, or Brussels sprouts. You may roast vegetables like broccoli, or Brussels sprouts – see recipe Day 4.

Fresh Fruit

Serves 4

Ingredients

- ¼ pound fruit per person

Directions

1. Wash, dry, and slice fruit onto a platter for serving.

Sample fruit combinations:

- Assorted berries like strawberries, blueberries, raspberries, and blackberries.
- Melon, like cantaloupe, and honeydew
- Exotic fruit, like mango, pineapple, and bananas
- Stone fruit, like plums, nectarines, peaches, and apricots.
- Fall fruit, like apples, bananas and pears.
- Winter fruit, like bananas, oranges, nectarines, and kiwi.

Nutrition varies by type of fruit

Course: Kitchen Primer: Dinner's Ready Day 3

Day 3 overview

Overview

Description

You will learn the importance of planning for meals in a day to help meet MyPlate guidelines for eating the recommended food groups. You will also learn about quick and nutrition ways to serve pasta.

Objectives

- Understand the basic components of a balanced meal
- Understand how planning for the meals in a day can help meet MyPlate guidelines for eating the recommended food groups
- Participants practice cooking techniques while preparing the menu for the day.

Everyone likes Pasta Menu

Pasta with seasonal sauce
Simple Salad
Italian Style Green Beans

What will we do today?

- Review MyPlate and the food groups
- Learn how to plan a balanced meal
- As a group discuss the case study and as a group complete the menu1 and menu2 comparison
- Prepare our menu
- Enjoy our menu

Sum of the Parts Equals a Meal

Overview

This lesson will teach what types of food make a plate healthy. Using 10 tips from the USDA MyPlate recommendations we will learn how to make a meal balanced, nutritious, and tasty.

What's A Balanced Plate?

If you are planning breakfast, lunch, or dinner, it is important to plan a balanced meal so that you get all nutrients your body needs to function properly. To make a balanced meal include at least one food from each of the following categories:

- Protein & Dairy, which include beans, nuts, meat, eggs, milk, and yogurt
- unrefined starches like whole grain bread or pasta
- Vitamin and mineral-rich foods, which include vegetables and fruit

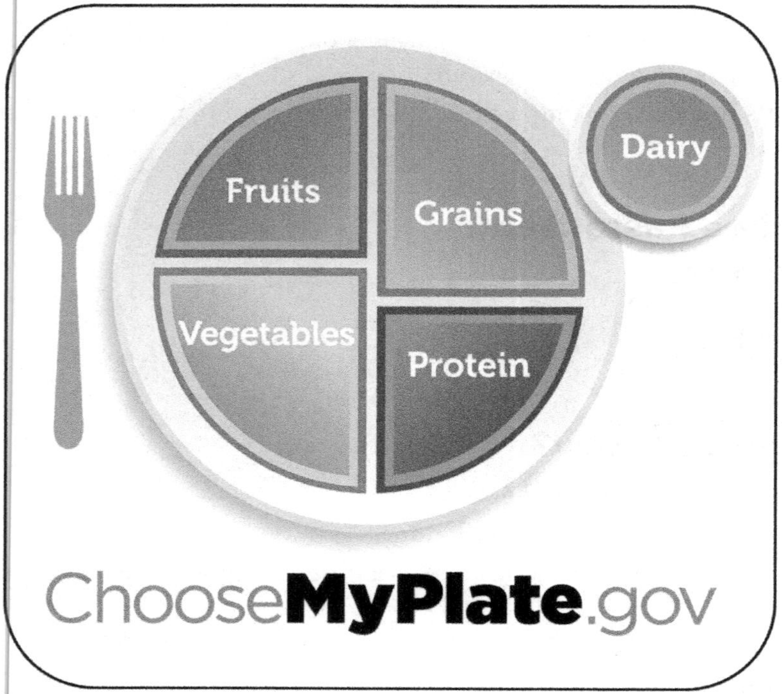

As a reminder here are the 5 basic food groups:

1) Dairy
2) Fruit
3) Grains
4) Protein Foods
5) Vegetables

Over the course of the day, make sure you have plenty of the various kinds of food so you stay healthy. You should eat breakfast, lunch, and dinner and sometimes snacks.

Most everyday family meals should be quick and easy, because everyone is busy going to work, school, and after-school activities. Dinners should include a salad, a main course, and a simple dessert. For special occasions and holidays, you might add appetizers, which are really a type of snack, and a fancier dessert.

Build A Healthy Meal Worksheet

10 tips
Nutrition Education Series

choose MyPlate

10 tips to a great plate

Making food choices for a healthy lifestyle can be as simple as using these 10 Tips.
Use the ideas in this list to *balance your calories*, to choose foods to *eat more often*, and to cut back on foods to *eat less often.*

1 balance calories
Find out how many calories YOU need for a day as a first step in managing your weight. Go to www.ChooseMyPlate.gov to find your calorie level. Being physically active also helps you balance calories.

2 enjoy your food, but eat less
Take the time to fully enjoy your food as you eat it. Eating too fast or when your attention is elsewhere may lead to eating too many calories. Pay attention to hunger and fullness cues before, during, and after meals. Use them to recognize when to eat and when you've had enough.

3 avoid oversized portions
Use a smaller plate, bowl, and glass. Portion out foods before you eat. When eating out, choose a smaller size option, share a dish, or take home part of your meal.

4 foods to eat more often
Eat more vegetables, fruits, whole grains, and fat-free or 1% milk and dairy products. These foods have the nutrients you need for health—including potassium, calcium, vitamin D, and fiber. Make them the basis for meals and snacks.

5 make half your plate fruits and vegetables
Choose red, orange, and dark-green vegetables like tomatoes, sweet potatoes, and broccoli, along with other vegetables for your meals. Add fruit to meals as part of main or side dishes or as dessert.

6 switch to fat-free or low-fat (1%) milk
They have the same amount of calcium and other essential nutrients as whole milk, but fewer calories and less saturated fat.

7 make half your grains whole grains
To eat more whole grains, substitute a whole-grain product for a refined product—such as eating whole-wheat bread instead of white bread or brown rice instead of white rice.

8 foods to eat less often
Cut back on foods high in solid fats, added sugars, and salt. They include cakes, cookies, ice cream, candies, sweetened drinks, pizza, and fatty meats like ribs, sausages, bacon, and hot dogs. Use these foods as occasional treats, not everyday foods.

9 compare sodium in foods
Use the Nutrition Facts label to choose lower sodium versions of foods like soup, bread, and frozen meals. Select canned foods labeled "low sodium," "reduced sodium," or "no salt added."

10 drink water instead of sugary drinks
Cut calories by drinking water or unsweetened beverages. Soda, energy drinks, and sports drinks are a major source of added sugar, and calories, in American diets.

United States Department of Agriculture
Center for Nutrition Policy and Promotion

Go to www.ChooseMyPlate.gov for more information.

DG TipSheet No. 1
June 2011
USDA is an equal opportunity provider and employer.

Optional Exercise

After reviewing MyPlate take a few minutes to write down a typical day's menu for you. If you need additional space, use the blank space at the bottom of the page.

Breakfast

What do you normally have for breakfast in the morning?

_______________ _______________ _______________

Lunch

What is a typical lunch you might eat during school?

_______________ _______________ _______________

Snack

Do you have a snack after school? What might you eat for a snack?

_______________ _______________

Dinner

What do you eat at dinner time?

_______________ _______________ _______________

Case Study – Checking your foods daily

Most of you are familiar with MyPlate and the different food groups. Today we will tie the food groups to our daily meals. Food is necessary to help us grow during childhood and teen years and to sustain adults. Food and water keep our body engine running. Eating the correct quantities throughout the day helps us stay healthy. It's important to understand how to eat throughout the day.

According to a sample MyPlate worksheet, a 7-year-old boy who exercises moderately is supposed to have the following foods daily:

5 oz. of grains	2 ½ cups of the milk group
2 cups of vegetables	5 oz. of the meat and bean group
1 ½ cups of fruits	

Note the following two menu choices and complete the exercises below.

1. Menu choice 1	**2. Menu choice 2**
a. Breakfast	a. Breakfast
• 1 pancake (2 oz.) with 2 tbsp. syrup	• breakfast cereal (2 oz)
• 1 cup of milk	• 1 cup of milk
b. Lunch	b. Lunch
• 1 turkey (2 oz.) sandwich on white bread (3 oz.) with mayonnaise	• 1 turkey (2 oz.) and cheese (1/4 cup) sandwich on whole wheat bread (3 oz.), slice of tomato, and piece of lettuce (1/4 cup)
• 1 bag of potato chips	• 1 apple
• 1 apple	• 1 oatmeal cookie (1/2oz.)
c. After school snack	c. After school snack
• 1 soda — 10 oz.	• 1 corn tortilla (1/2 oz.)
• 1 bag of corn chips	• Chopped peppers and onions (1/2 cup)
	• ¼ cup of cheese
d. Dinner	d. Dinner
• 2 pieces of fried chicken (6 oz.)	• Green salad (1/2 cup)
• French fries (1 cup)	• 1-piece roasted chicken (3 oz.)
• Broccoli (1/2 cup)	• Broccoli (¾ cup)
	• Baked potato (1/2 cup)
	• 1 cup of frozen yogurt

Case Study Questions

Exercise: Use the menu choices 1 and 2 to answer the following:

1. Does Menu 1 have a meal that has the three categories of food that make up a healthy plate? ______
2. List any of the foods in Menu 1 that represent the following food groups below.
   - Protein: ______________________________
   - Carbohydrate: ______________________________
   - Vitamin/Mineral-Rich Food: ______________________________
3. How many ounces of the protein group does Menu choice 1 have? ______
4. Does Menu 1 have any lean proteins?

   ____
5. What category of food is missing for dinner in Menu 1? ______
6. List a food that would make Menu1 dinner balanced.

   ____
7. Which meals from Menu 2 have a balanced plate?

   ____

   ____

   ____
8. What fruit is on Menu 2? ____________
9. What meal could you easily add fruit to?

   ____

   ____

   ____

10. How many ounces of the grain group does Menu choice 2 have?

____

11. What foods in Menu 2 are whole-grains?

____

____

12. How many servings are there from the dairy group in Menu 2?

____

13. What types of dairy foods should you choose to make a healthy plate?

____

____

14. Bonus: According to a sample MyPlate worksheet, a 7-year-old is supposed to have the following foods daily:

5 oz. of grains
2 cups of vegetables
1 ½ cups of fruits
2 1/2 cups of the milk group
5 oz. of the meat and bean group

15. Looking at the two menu choices, circle the one that meets the MyPlate recommendation for a 7-year-old boy?

Menu Choice 1 Menu Choice 2

P is for Pasta

Dry and fresh pasta

Pasta can be purchased fresh or dried. Typically, spaghetti is a dry pasta, while fettuccine is often found fresh. Generally Northern Italy uses more fresh pasta and Southern Italy uses more dry pasta.

Dry pastas are made using flour and water. The best dry pasta is made with the inner part of the wheat called durum, known as durum semolina when ground. The high gluten content in the flour helps the pasta soften yet remain firm when cooked, al dente.

Fresh pasta has a lighter texture because it is made with flour, eggs and water. It's not quite as easy to find fresh pasta as dried pasta. Wonton wrappers are pretty common in California and can be used as fresh pasta. Or, learn to make your own!

Cooking pasta

Bring a large pot of water to boil. Plan at least 4-5 quarts of water for 1 pound of pasta. Pasta will not cook properly if there is too little water. Traditionally, it is not necessary to add oil. Oil is sometimes added to ensure the pasta does not stick together; however, oil also will prevent the sauce from sticking to the pasta. So Chef-K does not recommend adding oil to pasta water.

When the water is boiling, add about 2-3 teaspoons of salt and then add the pasta. Give it a stir with a wooden spoon to prevent it from sticking.

Tasting the pasta is the best way to determine the doneness. Many packaged pasta instructions result in overcooked pasta, particularly because the pasta continues to cook as it is drained. Shape, size, fresh or dry all impact the cooking time needed. Strands like Cappelli or angel hair take only 1-2 minutes. Other dry pasta like pappardelle, spaghetti, rigatoni should be tested for doneness at five minutes. It should be firm, yet tender. The longest-cooking pastas should be done within 10-12 minutes.

Since pasta continues to cook, it is critical to drain it quickly, so have a colander in your clean sink ready to drain the instant it is al dente. Give the colander a couple of vigorous shakes to drain well and then pour into a serving bowl.

DAY 3: Let's Cook

Everyone likes Pasta

Menu

Pasta with seasonal sauce
Simple Salad
Italian Style Green Beans
Fresh Fruit

Game plan

1. Heat pot of water for blanching tomatoes
2. Prepare salad ingredients
3. Prepare green bean ingredients
4. Prepare ingredients for tomato sauce per recipe
5. Heat pot of water for pasta
6. Cook tomato sauce
7. Make Green Sauce
8. Cook Green beans
9. Cook pasta
10. Assemble salad
11. Drain pasta and add red sauce to ½ of cooked pasta
12. Add green sauce to other ½ of cooked pasta
13. Dress Salad
14. Serve meal

Recipe: Pasta with Red and Green Sauce

Red sauce – summer tomato

Makes 1 quart

Ingredients

- 4 pounds fresh ripe plum tomatoes
- 4 Tbsp olive oil
- 2 medium onions peeled and halved
- ¼ tsp salt
- ¼ tsp black pepper

Directions

1. Bring a large pot of water to boil
2. Blanch tomatoes in boiling water for about 3 minutes
3. Rinse in cold water, drain, and peel tomatoes
4. Cut tomatoes in half, remove seeds and chop
5. Add tomatoes to a heavy 5-quart saucepan over medium heat
6. Add olive oil, onion, salt and pepper
7. When it begins to bubble, reduce heat to low and simmer for 30-45 minutes
8. Break up tomatoes with potato masher or slotted spoon as they cook.
9. Discard onion
10. Taste and add salt and pepper as necessary.

Note: If desired, puree tomato to smoother sauce in a food processor or with an immersion blender. It's okay to puree onions with sauce at kid chef's discretion.

Winter Options:

You can replace fresh tomatoes with a 32 oz can of low salt whole tomatoes. Skip steps 1-5 of the directions if you use canned tomatoes.

You can also sauté some fresh mushrooms with a garlic clove and parsley to garnish the tomato sauce over pasta.

Nutritional Values

Nutrient name	Nutrient value	Unit
Calories	110	
Total Fat	10	g
Saturated Fat	1.5	g
Trans Fat	0	g
Cholesterol	0	mg
Sodium	75	mg
Carbohydrates	4	g
Dietary Fiber	<1	g
Sugars	3	g
Protein	<1	g
Vitamin A		IU
Vitamin C		mg
Calcium		mg
Iron		mg

This dish qualifies for USDA cholesterol free, and low sodium

Green Sauce (Pesto) – Summer only

Makes 1½ cups

This pesto is based on the traditional Genoa style. The traditional recipe includes pine nuts; however, you may substitute blanched almonds instead.

Ingredients

- 4 cups fresh basil leaves
- ¼ cup blanched almonds or pine nuts, optionally toasted
- 4 cloves garlic
- 1 tsp salt
- ¼ to ½ cup olive oil
- ¾ to 1 cup Parmesan or other dry cheese, grated

Directions

1. Gently wash and spin dry the basil leaves.
2. Put the basil, pine nuts, garlic, and salt in a blender or food processor.
3. Mix at high speed, periodically scraping down the sides, and slowly pour in olive oil until a fine paste is achieved.
4. Transfer the sauce to a small bowl and mix in cheese by hand until blended.

Note: If you would like to store basil for future use, it can be frozen. Here's how: purée only the basil leaves. Put the puréed basil in ice cube trays, pour olive oil over to cover, and freeze. Once the basil is frozen, transfer it to zippered plastic freezer bags. Each cube equals about 1 tablespoon of basil. Add the frozen cubes while sautéing vegetables or making soups or stews. You can thaw the cubes and add the remaining ingredients to make pesto.

Winter Options:

It's usually difficult to find fresh basil in non-summer months; so you will have to skip the pesto recipe.

Nutrition Facts

Nutrient name	Nutrient value	Unit
Calories	170	—
Total fat	16	g
Saturated fat	4	g
Trans fat	0	g
Cholesterol	10	mg
Sodium	590	mg
Carbohydrate	2	g
Dietary fiber	0	g
Sugars	0	g
Protein	6	g
Vitamin A	—	IU
Vitamin C	—	mg
Calcium	—	mg
Iron	—	mg

This dish qualifies for USDA low cholesterol, and sugar free.

Recipe: Pasta for 8

Ingredients

- 1-pound whole grain Fusilli or pappardelle or other small dry pasta with "pockets" or ridges. (or standard white flour pasta if whole grain is not available)
- 1 Tbsp olive oil
- 1/8 tsp salt and pepper to taste
- 2 Tbsp Parmesan cheese grated

From recipes above:

- ½ cup pesto
- 2 cups tomato sauce

Directions

1. Bring 6-8-quart pot of water to boil.
2. Add olive oil. Cook pasta 10-12 minutes. Usually package instructions overcook the pasta to my taste, so set timer for 2 minutes before package directions and taste. Pasta should be al dente (in other words has a little bite inside) Pasta continues to cook as you drain and prepare it.
3. When al dente, drain pasta in a large strainer.
4. Pour pasta into a bowl and add tomato sauce, salt and pepper and cheese to taste.

Nutrition Facts for standard white flour pasta

Nutrient name	Nutrient value	Unit
Calories	280	—
Total fat	9	g
Saturated fat	2	g
Trans fat	0	g
Cholesterol	5	mg
Sodium	160	mg
Carbohydrate	43	g
Dietary fiber	2	g
Sugars	1	g
Protein	9	g
Vitamin A	—	IU
Vitamin C	—	mg
Calcium	—	mg
Iron	—	mg

Nutrition Facts for whole grain pasta

Nutrient name	Nutrient value	Unit
Calories	280	—
Total fat	9	g
Saturated fat	2	g
Trans fat	0	g
Cholesterol	5	mg
Sodium	160	mg
Carbohydrate	42	g
Dietary fiber	6	g
Sugars	2	g
Protein	9	g
Vitamin A	—	IU
Vitamin C	—	mg
Calcium	—	mg
Iron	—	mg

When using whole grain pasta, this dish qualifies for USDA low cholesterol, and sugar free.

Recipe: Simple Salad

Serves 6

Ingredients

- ¼ red Italian-style torpedo onion (other sweet red onions are ok)
- 1 stalk celery
- 2 cups spring greens (about 8 oz)
- 1 small tomato or ½ basket of cherry tomatoes, or pear or apple diced in winter
- Salt (1/8 tsp to start)
- 2 Tbsp olive oil
- 2 Tbsp + 1 Tbsp red wine vinegar or white wine vinegar

Directions

1. Peel the onion and slice it in thin semicircles.
2. Place the onion in a small bowl, add 1 tablespoon of vinegar, and cover with cold water. Let it sit while you prepare the rest of the salad.
3. Wash and dry the celery and cut it into thin semicircles.
4. Wash the spring greens and spin them in a salad spinner or pat them dry with a paper towel.
5. Trim the spring greens, if needed.
6. Wash the tomato or fruit, and then cut in half and slice each half into pieces.
7. Drain the onions.
8. Put all of the ingredients into a large bowl.
9. When ready to serve, add salt and olive oil, and gently toss.
10. Sprinkle with vinegar, and gently toss once more.
11. Serve immediately.

Winter Options:

Eliminate tomato, replace with pear or apple.

Spring Options:

Eliminate tomato, replace with radishes.

Nutrition Facts

Nutrient name	Nutrient value	Unit
Calories	340	—
Total fat	28	g
Saturated fat	4	g
Trans fat	0	g
Cholesterol	0	mg
Sodium	410	mg
Carbohydrate	20	g
Dietary fiber	7	g
Sugars	10	g
Protein	6	g
Vitamin A	—	IU
Vitamin C	—	mg
Calcium	—	mg
Iron	—	mg

This dish qualifies for USDA low calories, low sodium, and cholesterol free.

Recipe: Italian-style Green Beans

Serves 6

The trick to tasty green beans is to choose beans that are smaller, bright green and firm. Larger beans that are not firm will be stringy and tough. Make sure to cook them just until they are tender but still a little firm.

Ingredients

- 1 pound green beans
- 2 Tbsp olive oil
- 1 clove garlic, minced (optional)
- Salt and pepper to taste (1/8 tsp of each to start)

Directions

1. Break off ends of beans and rinse in cold water.
2. Bring 3 quarts of water to a boil in a 4-5-quart pot.
3. Add the beans and pour in additional water if the beans are not completely covered. Cook until tender but still firm, about 4–5 minutes.
4. Drain the beans and place in a serving bowl.
5. Drizzle with olive oil and sprinkle with garlic, salt and pepper.

Note: If green beans are tough, you can blanch them in boiling water for a few minutes.

Nutritional Values

Nutrient name	Nutrient value	Unit
Calories	60	
Total Fat	4.5	g
Saturated Fat	0.5	g
Trans Fat	0	g
Cholesterol	0	mg
Sodium	55	mg
Carbohydrates	5	g
Dietary Fiber	3	g
Sugars	1	g
Protein	1	g
Vitamin A		IU
Vitamin C		mg
Calcium		mg
Iron		mg

This dish qualifies for USDA low calories, low saturated fat, low sodium, and cholesterol free.

Winter Options:

If green beans are not in season, you may be able to use broccoli, Swiss chard, kale, or Brussels sprouts. You may roast vegetables like broccoli, or Brussels sprouts – see recipe Day 4.

Fresh Fruit

Serves 4

Ingredients

- ¼ pound fruit per person

Directions

2. Rinse, dry, and slice fruit onto a platter for serving.

Sample fruit combinations:

- Assorted berries like strawberries, blueberries, raspberries, and blackberries.
- Melon, like cantaloupe, and honey dew
- Exotic fruit, like mango, pineapple, and bananas
- Stone fruit, like plums, nectarines, peaches, and apricots.
- Fall fruit, like apples, bananas, and pears.
- Winter fruit, like bananas, oranges, nectarines, and kiwi.

Nutrition varies by type of fruit

Course: Kitchen Primer: Dinner's Ready Day 4

Day 4 overview

Description

You will learn about common food allergies, and the causes and symptoms of a food allergy. You will learn the 8 foods that most often cause food allergies.

Objectives

After completing this class, you will be able to:

- describe what a food allergy is
- Become aware of what to look for on food labels as it pertains to food allergies
- Describe cooking food in the oven

Basic Roasted Meal Menu

Oven roasted chicken with potatoes

Roasted seasonal vegetables

What will we do today?

- Review top food allergies
- Learn about cooking in the oven
- Prepare our menu
- Enjoy our menu

Food Allergies

Today we are talking about food allergies. Are you allergic to anything? Is anyone in your household allergic to something? What kinds of things are they allergic to?

What is a food allergy?

A food allergy is an adverse reaction to a food or an ingredient in a food component that involves the body's immune system. Usually a protein causes a food allergy. It can be a serious condition and should be diagnosed by a board-certified allergist. A true food allergy (also called "food hypersensitivity") and its symptoms can take many forms. Common reactions are listed below, in the section titled "How to recognize a food allergy."

How does the body react to a food allergy?

A food allergy reaction usually occurs immediately or within 2 hours of contact with the offending food. Reactions can range from mild to life threatening. In a true food allergy, the body mistakenly identifies a food or a substance in food as a harmful substance, and the immune system forms antibodies to fight the culprit food or food substance (the allergen). The next time there is food contact, the antibodies release a chemical called histamine, as well as other chemicals, into your bloodstream. This leads to the allergic reaction. A person does not have to eat the food to experience an allergic reaction. Exposure to the food can be from inhalation, ingestion, or skin contact with the offending food.

What are the foods that most often cause food allergies?

There are 8 foods that most often cause allergies and generally these foods are high in protein. They are:

- milk
- eggs
- peanuts
- tree nuts (such as pecans or almonds)
- soy
- wheat
- fish
- shellfish

The most common childhood food allergy is milk although most outgrow this allergy by age three. The most serious allergic reactions are from peanuts and tree nuts. Allergies to peanuts and tree nuts are not generally outgrown.

Many of these foods are contained within other processed foods. It is very important to read the food labels on products to determine if any offending foods are contained within another product. For example, if a child was allergic to soy, products should be avoided that contain hydrolyzed soy protein, soy sauce, tofu, or textured vegetable protein. Even in very small amounts, an allergic reaction could occur if a person is exposed to these.

To help Americans avoid the health risks posed by food allergens, Congress passed the Food Allergen Labeling and Consumer Protection Act of 2004. This law requires that food labels must clearly identify the source of all ingredients that are — or are derived from — the eight most common food allergens. As a result, food labels will help allergic consumers to identify offending foods or ingredients so they can more easily avoid them.

Who is affected by food allergies?

Food allergy frequency is increasing in children. Currently about 4-8% of children have allergies. Infants under 2 years of age are more likely to develop food allergies but the incidence decreases with age. Some children grow out of food allergies. Factors that may increase chances for food allergies include heredity, exposure to allergens, gastrointestinal permeability, and environmental factors. About 2% of the adult population has food allergies.

How do you recognize a food allergy?

There are different types of allergic reactions to food. Allergic reactions can include:

- Hives
- Flushed skin or rash
- Tingling or itchy sensation in the mouth
- Face, tongue, or lip swelling
- Vomiting and/or diarrhea
- Coughing or wheezing
- Dizziness and/or lightheadedness
- Swelling of the throat and vocal cords
- Difficulty breathing
- Loss of consciousness
- Abdominal cramps

In rare cases of severe allergies, anaphylactic shock occurs. This includes multiple allergic reactions such as itching, hives, swelling of the throat, difficulty breathing, lower blood pressure, and loss of consciousness. Emergency medical treatment is needed immediately. Anaphylactic shock accounts for about 200 deaths per year.

What is the treatment for a food allergy?

The only way to avoid food allergies is to strictly avoid the offending food. Some children grow out of their allergies, so often a food that was once an allergy source may be reintroduced into the diet to determine if the allergic response is still active.

It is important to read all food labels carefully. A person that is severely allergic to certain foods should carry epinephrine, an important medication, with them at all times.

Tips to remember:

- Food allergies are serious. Don't make jokes about them.
- Don't share food with friends who have food allergies.
- Wash your hands after eating.
- Ask what your friends are allergic to, and help them avoid it.

Optional Group Activity

Do you ever look at the labels of the foods that you consume? By law, food packages must list all the ingredients in a product.

Ingredient lists tell you which ingredients are in the products you buy. This information is always printed on the outside of the package. Food ingredients are listed according to the amount of each ingredient in the package. The ingredient that weighs the most is listed first, and the ingredient that weighs the least is listed last.

Here is an example of an ingredient label for bread:

Whole Wheat Flour, Water, Wheat Gluten, Brown Sugar,
Molasses, Soybean Oil, Honey, Yeast, Salt, Cultured Wheat Starch, Oats, Soy Flour, Dough Conditioners.

Which ingredients may be a problem for people with food allergies? Which of the 8 foods that most often cause food allergies are contained in this bread?

What's in the oven?

Today we will be roasting meats and vegetables as well as baking some apples. Today we will be using the oven to prepare our meals. There are multiple styles of cooking in an oven. Here are a few:

- Roasting
- Baking
- Broiling

What is roasting?

As a young girl, the first meal I learned to make "all by myself" was roasted chicken with potatoes, onions and garlic served with a big green salad. It was an easy one pan meal. This became my specialty to make on Sundays, while my parents and brothers were out for the day.

Roasting is a specific method of baking food in the oven. It uses dry-heat with a minimum of fat, such as olive oil or butter at a high temperature. The only moisture is a bit that is naturally released from the food. The food will come out crisp and golden and flavorful.

Pans and heat

Meat should be roasted in a heavy metal roasting pans. Always use a roasting rack for meat so it does not steam in its own juices. Drain off some of the fat. Then deglaze the pan by pouring either lemon juice or wine to make a wonderful sauce to pour over the meat. Adding liquid to the pan lets you scrape up the brown bits and blends with the meat juices. This also makes it easier to clean the pan afterwards.

Vegetables should be roasted in either a heavy roasting pan or a heatproof glass baking dish with two- to three-inch sides. Use a pan that fits the amount of vegetables in a single layer. It's ok to layer the vegetables surrounding the meat rack. However, if you would like to reduce your intake of animal fat, place vegetables in a separate pan.

Day 4: Let's Cook

Basic Roasted Meal

Menu

Oven roasted chicken with potatoes

Roasted seasonal vegetables

Fresh fruit

Game plan

1. Preheat oven 425°
2. Prepare chicken
3. Place chicken in oven roast
4. Prepare vegetables, set aside
5. Prepare fruit and set aside
6. Add potatoes to chicken roasting pan (or a separate pan)
7. Prepare and roast seasonal vegetables
8. Remove chicken & vegetables let rest
9. Set table then carve chicken and serve meal
10. Clear table
11. Enjoy fresh Fruit

Recipe: Roasted Chicken With Potatoes, Onions and Garlic

Serves 12-15

This is the way my family always prepared chicken. It's the easiest and most straight forward way to cook a chicken.

A note from Laurie Zerga, founder of Chef-K

Ingredients

- 2 Whole chickens (4-7 pounds each.) Mary's or Organic chicken preferred
- 4-6 Tbsp olive oil divided
- 1 Tbs minced fresh rosemary or 1 teaspoon dried
- 4-6 garlic cloves minced
- 1/8 tsp salt & pepper
- 15 medium new potatoes or Yukon gold washed and quartered
- 2-3 medium onions peeled and quartered
- 8-9 whole garlic cloves peeled

Directions

1. Preheat oven to 425°
2. Remove neck and giblets from chicken. (Optional: reserve for making a quick stock)
3. Rinse chicken with cold water and pat dry with paper towels inside and out.
4. Salt and pepper body cavity.
5. Arrange on a roasting rack in a roasting pan
6. Brush the breast and legs with 2-3 Tbsp olive oil. Sprinkle with 1/8 tsp salt and pepper, and the rosemary
7. Brush minced garlic over chicken.
8. Place potatoes, onion and whole garlic around chicken and drizzle 2-3 Tbsp olive oil over vegetables. Salt and pepper to taste.
9. It will take 50-75 minutes to roast, depending on the size of the chicken. Use an instant-read meat thermometer to prick the thickest part of the thigh. It should register 160-170°. If the temperature is allowed to go higher; it will dry out the breast meat.
10. Remove chicken to a platter to let rest for 10-15 minutes; it will continue to cook from its own heat.
11. Remove leg & thighs & wings. Then carve breast and place on warm platter.
12. Place potatoes in a serving casserole and leave in warm oven.

Nutritional Values

Nutrient name	Nutrient value	Unit
Calories	560	
Total Fat	32	g
Saturated Fat	9	g
Trans Fat	0	g
Cholesterol	130	mg
Sodium	130	mg
Carbohydrates	32	g
Dietary Fiber	4	g
Sugars	2	g
Protein	34	g
Vitamin A		IU
Vitamin C		mg
Calcium		mg
Iron		mg

This dish qualifies for USDA low sodium.

Pan Gravy (optional)

Ingredients

- 1/4 cup fresh lemon juice
- 1/2 cup chicken stock or broth
- Drippings from the roasting pan

Directions

1. Drain off excess fat. Then place pan with drippings on stove burner.
2. Add wine or lemon juice, scraping up brown bits at bottom of pan.
3. Add chicken stock and bring to boil.
4. Reduce the heat and let simmer 10-15 minutes to reduce to a rich sauce.

Recipe: Roasted Vegetables

Excellent vegetables to roast include:

- Asparagus (10 minutes)
- Broccoli, (20 minutes)
- Brussels Sprouts (15 minutes)
- Cauliflower (20 minutes)
- Eggplant (sliced, 15 minutes)
- Kale (sliced, 10 minutes)
- Onions (sliced, 15 minutes)
- Peppers (15 minutes)
- Potatoes (40 minutes)
- Zucchini (1-inch pieces, 15 minutes)

Drizzle with:

- 2 Tbsp olive oil
- ¼ tsp each salt and pepper

Directions

1. Preheat oven 400°
2. Rinse, dry, and slice vegetable of choice as desired
3. Drizzle 1-2 Tbsp olive oil over vegetables and roast for time specified above.

Note: try other herbs such as oregano or rosemary on potatoes or zucchini, or dill on cauliflower. Experiment!

Sample vegetable combinations:

- Broccoli and cauliflower.
- Beets and Zucchini (this is an unexpected combination and quite tasty)
- Carrots and cauliflower
- Carrots and Brussels sprouts
- Corn and peppers
- Zucchini, eggplant, and peppers

Nutrition information varies based on vegetables used.

Fresh Fruit

Serves 4

Ingredients

- ¼ pound fruit per person

Directions

Rinse , dry, and slice fruit onto a platter for serving.

Sample fruit combinations:

- Assorted berries like strawberries, blueberries, raspberries, and blackberries.
- Melon, like cantaloupe, and honeydew
- Exotic fruit, like mango, pineapple, and bananas
- Stone fruit, like plums, nectarines, peaches, and apricots.
- Fall fruit, like apples, bananas, and pears.
- Winter fruit, like bananas, oranges, nectarines, and kiwi.

Nutrition varies by type of fruit

Course: Kitchen Primer: Dinner's Ready Day 5

Day 5 overview

Description

Celebrate what you have learned and enjoy a buffet.

Objectives

- Prepare a celebration buffet

Mexican Fiesta Menu

Turkey Tacos
Shredded Cheese
Guacamole
Salsa Fresca
Tortilla Chips
Warm Corn & Flour Tortillas
Calabacitas with Corn and Tomatoes
Fresh Fruit

What will we do today?

- Plan and prepare our celebration
- Prepare our menu
- Enjoy our dinner

Day 5: Let's Cook

Mexican Fiesta

Menu

Turkey Tacos
Guacamole
Salsa Fresca
Tortilla Chips
Calabacitas with Corn and Tomatoes
Fresh Fruit

Game plan

1. Prepare the vegetables for calabacitas and set aside.
2. Prepare the fruit for dessert.
3. Prepare salsa and guacamole, cover and set on table.
4. Prepare Turkey Tacos
5. Set the table and set out drinks.
6. Set out a buffet of food and serve.
7. Clear dishes from the table.

Recipe: Basic Table Salsa (Salsa Fresca)

Makes 1 ½ cups
Serves 8

Ingredients

- 2 large, firm red-ripe tomatoes seeded (or fresh cranberries in winter)
- 1 clove garlic peeled
- 1 Anaheim or California green chili seeded
- 3 green onions trimmed and chopped, or 1/3 cup chopped red onion
- 1 tsp olive oil
- 1 Tbsp fresh lime juice or wine vinegar
- ¼ tsp salt, or to taste
- Cracked black pepper
- 1 Tbsp chopped cilantro (optional)

Directions

1. Chop tomatoes and place in bowl.
2. Chop, garlic, chili, and onions together then add to tomatoes. (All ingredients should be chopped either by hand, in a blender, or food processor until desired consistency.)
3. Mix in green chilies, olive oil, lime juice, salt, pepper and cilantro.
4. Allow flavors to develop for 1 hour, and then serve.

Nutritional Values

Nutrient name	Nutrient value	Unit
Calories	20	
Total Fat	1.5	g
Saturated Fat	0	g
Trans Fat	0	g
Cholesterol	0	mg
Sodium	75	mg
Carbohydrates	1	g
Dietary Fiber	0	g
Sugars	< 1	g
Protein	0	g
Vitamin A	--	IU
Vitamin C	--	mg
Calcium	--	mg
Iron	--	mg

This dish qualifies for USDA low calories, free of saturated fat, and cholesterol free.

Winter Options:

Note: During winter – try replacing tomatoes with a 12 oz bag of fresh cranberries

Recipe: Guacamole

Makes 1 cup
Serves 8

Ingredients

- 4 ripe avocados mashed (if unavailable look for frozen avocados)
- 1 Tbsp fresh lime juice (or lemon if lime is not available, a combination is also fine)
- Salt & pepper to taste

Directions

1. Combine all ingredients.
2. To store, cover tightly with plastic wrap so that the avocadoes do not get dark and are less appetizing (It is okay to prepare several hours ahead and possibly the night before).

Nutritional Values

Nutrient name	Nutrient value	Unit
Calories	160	
Total Fat	15	g
Saturated Fat	2	g
Trans Fat	0	g
Cholesterol	0	mg
Sodium	25	mg
Carbohydrates	9	g
Dietary Fiber	7	g
Sugars	< 1	g
Protein	2	g
Vitamin A	--	IU
Vitamin C	--	mg
Calcium	--	mg
Iron	--	mg

This dish qualifies for USDA low sodium, and cholesterol free.

Recipe: Calabacitas with Corn and Tomatoes

Serves 6

Ingredients

- 3 Tbsp olive oil
- ½ medium onion, peeled and sliced into eighths
- 1 garlic clove peeled and coarsely chopped
- 1 yellow summer squash sliced 1-inch thick
- 1 small zucchini squash sliced 1-inch thick
- 3 green onions sliced
- ½ cup fresh or frozen corn kernels (from t 1 to 2 ears of fresh corn)
- 1 mild green chili, roasted, peeled, seeded, and cut into pieces
- 2 plum (Roma) tomatoes, quartered and seeded
- ⅛ tsp salt and pepper, or to taste

Directions

1. Pre heat oven to 400°F
2. Place onion, garlic, and squash on a roasting tray or pan
3. Roast 20 minutes
4. Stir in the remaining vegetables
5. Roast 10 minutes longer

Alternative cooking method:

1. Heat oil in a large skillet.
2. Sauté onion until softened, 3-4 minutes.
3. Add garlic and sauté 2 minutes more.
4. Add the sliced squash and sauté for 5 minutes until softened.
5. Stir in the green onions, corn, and green chili and sauté for 3 more minutes.
6. Stir in the tomato. Remove from heat.
7. Season with salt and pepper, and then divide into 6 equal portions to serve.

Vegetables should be tender but not mushy or crunchy.

Winter Options:

In winter, instead of zucchini and yellow squash; use butternut, or acorn squash. Peel and cube the squash and use it to replace the summer squash. Frozen corn kernels can be used instead of fresh corn.

Nutrition Facts

Nutrient name	Nutrient value	Unit
Calories	140	—
Total fat	8	g
Saturated fat	1	g
Trans fat	0	g
Cholesterol	0	mg
Sodium	110	mg
Carbohydrate	16	g
Dietary fiber	3	g
Sugars	3	g
Protein	3	g
Vitamin A	—	IU
Vitamin C	—	mg
Calcium	—	mg
Iron	—	mg

This dish qualifies for USDA low calories, low saturated fat, low sodium, and cholesterol free.

Recipe: Turkey Tacos

Serves 6

Ingredients

- ½ pound ground turkey
- 1 Tbsp olive oil
- ½ onion, diced
- 1 garlic clove
- 1 8oz can tomato sauce
- 1 tsp ground cumin
- 1 tsp chili powder
- ¾ cup shredded Monterey jack or cheddar cheese
- 2 Tbsp chopped cilantro
- Salt and pepper to taste (1/4 tsp to start)
- 6 whole wheat tortillas – fajita size (30 g each) or try corn tortillas

Directions

1. Heat a large non-stick pan over medium heat
2. Add olive oil and onion.
3. Sauté onion until translucent, 3-4 minutes
4. Add ground turkey and sauté until browned (3-5 minutes)
5. Add garlic and sauté 1 minute more
6. Add tomato sauce, cumin, chili powder, salt and pepper.
7. Simmer 10 minutes.
8. Layer tortillas on a baking sheet and cover with aluminum foil place in oven for 10 minutes while meat is simmering.
9. Spoon approximately 1/3 cup meat mixture per tortillas.
10. Garnish with 2 Tbsp cheese and cilantro

Nutritional Values

Nutrient Name	Nutrient Value	Unit
Calories	320	
Total Fat	18	g
Saturated Fat	7	g
Trans Fat	0	g
Cholesterol	65	mg
Sodium	540	mg
Carbohydrates	17	g
Dietary Fiber	9	g
Sugars	2	g
Protein	21	g
Vitamin A		IU
Vitamin C		mg
Calcium		mg
Iron		mg

Fresh Fruit

Serves 4

Ingredients

- ¼ pound fruit per person

Directions

1. Rinse, dry, and slice fruit onto a platter for serving.

Sample fruit combinations:

- Assorted berries like strawberries, blueberries, raspberries, and blackberries.
- Melon, like cantaloupe, and honeydew
- Exotic fruit, like mango, pineapple, and bananas
- Stone fruit, like plums, nectarines, peaches, and apricots.
- Fall fruit, like apples and pears.
- Winter fruit, like oranges, nectarines, and kiwi.

Nutrition varies by type of fruit

Appendix A: Glossary of Terms

These are some common terms you may run across in recipes. Many are used in the class recipes.

Baking	A general term meaning to cook food in the oven. There are several different ways to cook food in the oven. Dry hot heat over 400°F is typically called **roasting.** A lower temperature of 350°F is usually referred to as baking.
Blanching	A general term means cooking the ingredient just to soften the food a bit for easier processing or eating. It might be used for cured meats (salt pork) to reduce the saltiness. Often vegetables or fruit are blanched in order to allow the skin to be peeled before processing further. The basic technique is to bring a pot of water to boil and then place the ingredient into the boiling water for a short amount of time. The amount of time varies by ingredient. Sometimes blanching is also called **parboiling**.
Brown	Browning is a cooking technique that allows a meat or vegetable to become seared quickly over medium high heat. Usually it gets brown marks from the heat of the pan. Typically, after browning, liquid is added to the pan to bring up flavors from the bits attached to the pan. The ingredient is then simmered slowly to finish cooking.
Chop	Cutting into rough pieces. You can chop coarsely (into big pieces) or finely (into small pieces).
Dice	To cut food into tiny (about 1/8- to 1/4-inch) cubes.
Grill	A method of quickly searing meat over a barbeque or in a special pan to give the meat brown marks.
Ice bath	An ice bath is a quick way to cool off a pot that has been on the stove for a while. It is used prior to placing the pot into the refrigerator. Placing a hot pot into a refrigerator may bring the temperature of all stored items too high. Cool by plunging the pot into a pan or sink full of water and ice so that the pot is covered half way up. Stir the contents of the pot to cool it down; be careful that the water is not too high up the side of pot because you don't want water to get into cooked ingredients.
Julienne	Foods that have been cut into very thin, matchstick strips. The food is first cut into 1/8-inch-thick slices. The slices are stacked, and then cut into 1/8-inch-thick strips. The strips may then be cut into whatever length is desired.
Mince	To cut into very small pieces, smaller than chopped

Pickle Pickling is a way to prepare vegetables soaked in an acidic liquid, like vinegar or lemon juice. The acid in the liquid softens the vegetable over a period of time. Vegetables can be pickled by letting them marinade without heat. However, in the case of "pickles" the vegetable is processed with heat in jars in a special way so that the vegetable is preserved for a long period of time, up to 1 year or longer. Cucumbers, carrots, onions, and radishes are common vegetables that are pickled.

Poach Poaching is a method of cooking an ingredient, such as meat or vegetables by slowly simmering in warm liquid with herbs and spices until cooked. Typical poaching liquids are broth, wine or water.

Roasting Dry hot heat over 400°F is typically called **roasting.**

Roux Roux is a mixture of equal parts flour and butter or other fat that is slowly stirred in a pan over low heat until it is lightly toasted. It is used to thicken sauces and soups.

Sauté Sautéing is a cooking technique in which food is cooked quickly in a small amount of oil or other fat in a skillet or sauté pan over direct heat.

Sear A method of cooking quickly over high heat to seal in juices and flavor of an ingredient. It is typically used as a technique for meat and poultry.

Soft-ball stage Soft ball stage is a reference for candy-making and jam. It refers to the point when the sugar is melted and combined with other ingredients and then starts to thicken. When the mixture reaches a temperature 238-240°F the melted sugar should be able to form a small ball. Test by dropping a bit of melted sugar mixture into a glass of ice water, it should cling together and when removed from the water, it can be rolled into a tiny ball.

Trinity Onions, green pepper and celery are called the *trinity* and are the basis for almost every Creole and Cajun recipe.

Appendix B: Check what you learned

For your convenience, a comprehensive quiz for the week is provided. You may wish to use this "Check what you've learned" for tracking purposes.

Dinner's Ready: Check what you've learned

NAME____________________ DATE_________

Questions:
True/False – respond true or false to the following questions:

1. When passing a knife to another person; always present the blade or tip to them.
2. There are 8 common food allergies that we reviewed this week.
3. Always make sure a knife is clean and dry before using it.
4. It's a good idea to use the blade to scrape food off of a cutting board.
5. It's best to leave a soiled knife in warm soapy water while you prepare the rest of your meal.
6. Always use a cutting board to protect your counter or table top.
7. If a knife falls it's best to try to catch it before it hits the ground.
8. Dice and chop are sometimes used interchangeably in recipes.
9. Refrigerate or freeze perishables, prepared food, and leftovers within two hours.
10. It is important to cook meats, fish, and poultry correctly to ensure that all bacteria are killed.
11. It's a good idea to read food labels; especially if you have food allergies.

Multiple choice – select the best answer from a to c

1. A good way to store a knife is:
   a. Laying flat in a drawer with a knife guard
   b. In a knife block
   c. Both a. & b. are good ways to store knives.

2. Always keep your knife sharp. The following helps to keep the knife sharp.
    a. Never scrape food off a cutting board with the blade.
    b. Never use a knife for anything except for cutting.
    c. All of the above.

3. It is important in food safety to
    a. Plan, Find, Gather, Cook, Serve,
    b. Clean, Separate, Cook, and Chill

4. Which of the following are common food allergens?
    a. Soy
    b. Milk
    c. Peanuts.
    d. All of the above

Fill in the blank for the following questions:

1. Dry heat over 400°F is typically called ___________

2. _________ refers to food cut into tiny (about 1/8- to 1/4-inch) cubes.

3. USDA recommends you make ________ of your plate fruits and vegetables.

4. __________ is a method of cooking that allows a meat or vegetable to become seared quickly over medium heat.

5. ___________refers to foods that have been cut into very thin, matchstick strips

6. Can you name the four meals typically eaten throughout the day?

a.______________________________

b.______________________________

c.______________________________

d.______________________________

7. If you are a 10-year-old boy or girl, MyPlate recommends you eat 2½ cups of vegetables a day. When would you eat your vegetables?

8. What are three types of food you need on a healthy plate?

a.______________________________

b.______________________________

c.______________________________

9. According to USDA how much of your grains should be whole grains?

____

10. What type of grains can be part of a healthy plate?

____

11. What are two ways you can reduce the amount of fat you eat?

a.____

b.____

12. Name three high protein foods that would fit on a healthy plate?

a.______________________________

b.______________________________

c.______________________________

12. Which of the following are common food allergies?
   a. eggs
   b. fruit
   c. milk

13. Casein is another name for:

   e. wheat
   f. milk
   g. fish
   h. soy

14. If you have a food allergy, you should read food labels.

   True or False

15. Almonds are a type of ____ that many people are allergic to.

   d. tree nut
   e. soy
   f. fish

Appendix C: Optional Desserts

Recipe: Basic Fruit Brown Betty – use any season

Serves 12

Ingredients

- 4-5 cups sliced fruit (1 ½ pounds) (see suggestions below by season)
- ¼ cup coconut oil or unsalted butter + 2 Tbsp
- ¼ cup fresh lemon juice
- 2 Tbsp brown sugar
- 1 cup dates pitted and chopped - optional
- 1 ¼ cup whole wheat flour
- 1 ½ cup old fashioned or quick-cooking oatmeal
- 1 tsp ground cinnamon
- ½ tsp salt
- ¼ cup water

Directions

1. Preheat oven 350°
2. Use 2 Tbsp of coconut oil or butter to grease inside 13- x 9-inch inch heatproof glass baking dish
3. Rinse, , drain, and slice fruit
4. Place fruit in baking dish
5. Pour lemon juice over fruit and toss gently
6. Melt butter in a medium bowl in microwave for 30-60 seconds. (Alternatively, melt in a medium pot on top of the stove.)
7. Add brown sugar, flour, oatmeal, cinnamon and salt to the melted butter. Mixture should be crumbly and resemble coarse pebbles.
8. Crumble topping evenly over fruit
9. Place in oven and bake for 50-60 minutes, until the fruit is tender, and the topping is golden brown.
10. Serve warm with vanilla ice cream or crème fraiche. (optional)

Nutritional Values

Nutrient Name	Nutrient Value	Unit
Calories	160	
Total Fat	6	g
Saturated Fat	4	g
Trans Fat	0	g
Cholesterol	0	mg
Sodium	100	mg
Carbohydrates	22	g
Dietary Fiber	4	g
Sugars	0	g
Protein	5	g
Vitamin A		IU
Vitamin C		mg
Calcium		mg
Iron		mg

This dish qualifies for USDA cholesterol-free using coconut oil

Nutrition varies with fruit added.

Summer Fruit

Nectarines, plums, peaches are great choices

Fall

Apples or pears

Winter

Use frozen fruit such as berries, peaches, or other fruit. Apples are also often available in winter.

Spring

Berries are wonderful in the spring and early summer, raspberries and also rhubarb is good. Note: Rhubarb, plums, or other tart fruit may require extra sugar.

Recipe: Cannon Banana Surprise – use in winter or spring

This recipe was created during our class at Cannon AFB March 2012.

Ingredients

Serves 4

- 5 Bananas
- 1 Tbsp Brown Sugar

Directions

1. Preheat oven to 400. Line a 13- x 9-inch baking sheet with parchment paper or aluminum foil.
2. Peel bananas
3. Cut banana's in half, crosswise
4. Cut banana halves in half again
5. tt Arrange banana pieces on the prepared baking sheet
6. Sprinkle brown sugar on bananas
7. Pat brown sugar down if needed to cling to the bananas.
8. Bake for 10 minutes, or until the bananas are heated through and the topping is crunchy.

Nutritional Values

Nutrient Name	Nutrient Value	Unit
Calories	140	
Total Fat	0	g
Saturated Fat	0	g
Trans Fat	0	g
Cholesterol	0	mg
Sodium	0	mg
Carbohydrates	37	g
Dietary Fiber	4	g
Sugars	21	g
Protein	2	g
Vitamin A		IU
Vitamin C		mg
Calcium		mg
Iron		mg

This dish qualifies for USDA low calories, low fat, and saturated fat-free, cholesterol-free, sodium free

Recipe: Banana Freeze – use in summer

This recipe was created during our class at Tinker AFB July 2012.

Ingredients

Serves 4

- 5 Bananas
- 1 cup strawberries or mixed fresh seasonal berries
- 2 Tbs. unsweetened cocoa powder or semi-sweet chocolate chips, optional
-

Directions

1. Cut bananas into slices – place in the freezer in a zip lock bag for 1-2 hours.
2. Place berries in a saucepan over medium-high heat.
3. Cook berries for about 10 minutes to make a sauce., Set aside until ready to serve
4. Remove bananas from freezer and puree in a food processor or blender.
5. Place a scoop of frozen banana puree in individual bowls
6. Top each scoop with 2 Tbsp of the reserved berry sauce
7. If cocoa or chocolate chips are available, sprinkle on top.

Nutritional Values

Nutrient Name	Nutrient Value	Unit
Calories	150	
Total Fat	1	g
Saturated Fat	0	g
Trans Fat	0	g
Cholesterol	0	mg
Sodium	0	mg
Carbohydrates	38	g
Dietary Fiber	5	g
Sugars	20	g
Protein	2	g
Vitamin A		IU
Vitamin C		mg
Calcium		mg
Iron		mg

This dish qualifies for USDA low calories, low fat, and saturated fat-free, cholesterol-free, sodium free

Recipe Very Berry Cobbler – use in winter

Serves 12

This recipe was created during our class at Cannon AFB March 2012.

Ingredients

- 1 ½ sticks (3/4 cup) unsalted butter
- 1 1/2 cups dried mixed fruit (such as prunes, apricots, and pear) or 6 oz. dried blueberries
- 1 1/2 cups raisins or 6 oz. sweetened dried cranberries
- 1 1/2 cups pitted and sliced dates (about 6 oz)
- Juice of 1 orange (1/4 cup)
- 1/4 cup brown sugar
- 1 cup (whole wheat) flour
- 3/4 cup old fashioned or quick-cooking rolled oats
- 1 1/2 tsp vanilla extract, optional
- 1 tsp. Ground cinnamon

Directions

1. Preheat oven to 350
2. Grease a13- x 9- inch baking dish with 1 Tbsp butter
3. Mix dry fruit in bowl
4. Squeeze orange juice over the fruit
5. Combine remaining butter, flour, oats, vanilla (if using) and cinnamon in a separate bowl, set aside
6. Spread fruit mixture in the prepared baking dish
7. Crumble oat mixture over top of fruit
8. Place i for 20 minutes, until the fruit is tender, and the topping is golden

Nutritional Values

Nutrient Name	Nutrient Value	Unit
Calories	230	
Total Fat	5	g
Saturated Fat	2.5	g
Trans Fat	0	g
Cholesterol	10	mg
Sodium	5	mg
Carbohydrates	45	g
Dietary Fiber	5	g
Sugars	18	g
Protein	4	g
Vitamin A		IU
Vitamin C		mg
Calcium		mg
Iron		mg

This dish qualifies for USDA low sodium, low cholesterol

Notes

96154516R00089

Made in the USA
Columbia, SC
23 May 2018